# The Bliss Seekers

*Bridging the Gap
Between You and Your Spouse*

Richard Nicholson

All rights reserved. This book or any portion thereof may not be reproduced or used in any manner whatsoever without the express written permission of the author.

Scripture quotations taken from:

(AMP) *The Amplified New Testament*, © 1954, 1958, 1987 by The Lockman Foundation. Used by permission.

(ESV) *The Holy Bible, English Standard Version*. Copyright © 2001 by Crossway Bibles, a publishing ministry of Good News Publishers.

(KJV) *The Holy Bible*, King James Version.

(MSG) THE MESSAGE. Copyright © 1993, 1994, 1995. Used by permission of NavPress Publishing Group.

(NASB)*The New American Standard Bible*, © 1960, 1962, 1963, 1968, 1971, 1972, 1973, 1975, 1977 by The Lockman Foundation. Used by permission.

(NIV) *HOLY BIBLE, New International Version®*, NIV®, copyright © 1973, 1978, 1984, 2011 by Biblica Inc. Used by permission. All rights reserved worldwide.

(NLT) The *Holy Bible*, New Living Translation, copyright © 1996. Used by permission of Tyndale House Publishers, Inc., Wheaton, IL 60189. All rights reserved.

Printed in the United States of America
Kindle Direct Publishing
First Printing: 2019

Copyright © 2019 Richard Nicholson

Cover and Interior Design by C.A. Simonson

ISBN: 9781096553137

# TABLE OF CONTENTS

**Preface** ............................................................................................. 9

**Chapter One:** ................................................................................ 13
  **What Is Marital Bliss and How Can We Find It?** ............ 13
    TOOLS WE CAN USE ............................................................ 15
    MARRIAGE CAN BE EXCELLENT ........................................ 15
    ON-THE-JOB TRAINING WITH HELP FROM MY FRIENDS 16
    THE WIFE AS A FITTING HELPER ....................................... 17
    WHAT MARRIAGE IS NOT .................................................. 18
    THE DNA OF MARRIAGE .................................................... 19
  **Marriage Is a Mystery** ................................................................ 24
  **Marriage Is a Challenge** ............................................................ 26
  **Marriage Is a Cause** ................................................................... 29

**Chapter Two:** ................................................................................ 34
  **A Scriptural Model for a Healthy Marriage** ................... 34
    THE TOP-DOWN MODEL: A VERTICAL VIEW ................. 34
    THE EGALITARIAN MODEL: A HORIZONTAL VIEW ...... 37
    IS THERE CLEAR BIBLE TEACHING ON THE SUBJECT? ... 39
    ONE HISTORICAL VIEW BY A SPANIARD ........................ 46
    CONTEMPORARY VIEWS ON SUBMISSION AND
    EQUALITY ............................................................................ 48
    ARE BASIC FAMILY VALUES RELEVANT TODAY? .......... 51

**Chapter Three:** ............................................................................. 53
  **Guiding Principles for Connecting to the Right Mate**. 53
    LEAVING ............................................................................... 54
    CLEAVING ............................................................................ 61
    JOINED ................................................................................. 65
    INSEPARABLE ...................................................................... 66

**Chapter Four:** ............................................................................... 71
  **Affection Wins** ............................................................................ 71
    # 1. KINDNESS IS THE SUPERPOWER ............................. 71
    # 2. ROMANCE STOKES THE FIRE .................................... 78

**Chapter Five:** ............................................................................ **81**
   **Intimacy** ................................................................................ **81**
      # 3. SEXUAL INTIMACY KEEPS US IN TUNE WITH EACH OTHER ................................................................................. 81
      # 4. PHYSICAL TOUCH HELPS BONDING .......................... 89
      # 5. PLACE YOUR SPOUSE HIGHER ON THE LADDER OF LIFE ................................................................................. 93

**Chapter Six:** ............................................................................. **102**
   **Conquering the Giants** ...................................................... **102**
      # 6. OVERCOME ANGER, ABUSE, AND ADULTERY ..... 102

**Chapter Seven:** ....................................................................... **124**
   **Nurturing Intimacy with Your Spouse** ......................... **124**
      # 7. RECOGNIZE "BIDS" AND LEAN TOWARD YOUR SPOUSE ............................................................................. 124
      # 8. LEARN A NEW LANGUAGE ......................................... 128
      # 9. INCLUDE YOUR SPOUSE IN DAILY DECISIONS .... 138

**Chapter Eight:** ......................................................................... **143**
   **Emotional and Spiritual Intimacy** .................................. **143**
      # 10. PRAY TOGETHER ........................................................ 143
      # 11. PLAY TOGETHER ........................................................ 145
      # 12. CONNECT BY TALKING FROM THE HEART ........ 148
      # 13. ENDURE AND PROCESS SUFFERING WELL ........ 156
      # 14. DISCOVER A COMMON MISSION, PURPOSE, OR DESTINY ........................................................................... 158
      # 15. TIE UP LOOSE ENDS: THE BUCKET LIST ............. 164
      # 16. RESET-A FRESH START AND A CLEAN SLATE .. 170

**ABOUT THE AUTHOR** ........................................................... **177**

# Acknowledgements

Any creative project such as writing a book is almost always one that banks on the input, encouragement, and direction of many people. For the *Bliss Seekers,* I am indebted to my wife and lifetime partner, Cynthia, who not only encouraged me but also gave me her top-tier coaching to help make this book a reality. In addition, she models many of the positive aspects of relationship building that sets the bar higher for me every day.

Two individuals suggested early on that I write and nudged me toward that end, and two other true friends, Dr. Floyd "Butch" Frey and his wife, Pam, were the first to read some of the rough original manuscripts and stimulated me by their affirmations to keep moving forward. I can't adequately thank them enough for those initial encouraging words.

It was Dr. Frey who recommended my first editor, Linda Triemstra of Gold Leaf Editorial Services, who was amazing in her professionalism combined with kindness that helped me walk this book into reality.

Finally C.A. Simonson took the book across the finish line with her expertise and enthusiasm for publishing.

I owe my wife and all of these friends, believers who are gifted and themselves God's gifts to others, for their heart for those things that really matter in life—how we relate to those around us as we journey forward.

# The Bliss Seekers

*Bridging the Gap
Between You and Your Spouse*

# Preface

Have you ever committed a relational blunder with friends or family, then wondered, "Why didn't I know I was blowing it? Why didn't someone tell me?" I have, too, and most of the time it's embarrassing. Marriage can be like that, a classic trial-and-error effort.

But is trial and error the only way to succeed in marriage? Are there not proven ways to insure growth and satisfaction as a married couple? I believe there are practices and habits that will maximize the possibility of success in any relationship and especially in marriage. That is what this book is all about.

Simply put, the key to marriage success is to understand that there is considerable distance between an individual and their spouse at the beginning of their relationship, though they may not realize it at the beginning. Additionally, the lack of awareness of how much distance there is between the husband and wife tends to cloud the reality that marriage is a marathon, not a sprint. If you want to go the distance, you will need ongoing strategies that work. The very phrase "the two shall become one" implies closing the distance, a merging and uniting. It is a process.

Often, that cloud cover over the reality of living together as a couple is slow to evaporate because the concept of being "in love" implies that love is the only ingredient that matters. In one sense it is, but the love that endures, that is true love, has many components, and each one serves to stabilize and reinforce the relationship between two people. Married life is a result of both loving and learning.

Therefore the prime requirement for marital success is finding ways to close that gap between both spouses by a lifetime of discovery, improvement, correction, and the application of the knowledge gained to help them navigate the troubled seas of relationships in today's culture. If you both love and learn, you stand a great chance of living happily ever after!

We trust that the recommendations in this book will spark in you a deep desire to break free from any stalemate and release in your lives all that is really necessary to truly live happily ever after.

# PART ONE

## SETTING THE STAGE FOR SUCCESS IN MARRIAGE

# CHAPTER ONE:
## What Is Marital Bliss and How Can We Find It?

Ahhh, marital bliss, if only we could find it... wait a minute. Just what is this thing called "bliss" anyway? People refer to "marital bliss," but isn't that just like falling in love? And we've heard of "eternal bliss," especially at funerals. But we've also heard people say, "Ignorance is bliss."

Interestingly enough, this Old English word *bliss* has been around for about eight centuries at least. So what does the word mean, and is it relevant to my spouse and me? Let's unpack this concept of marital or wedded bliss. According to the Merriam-Webster dictionary, bliss can be

1. A state of complete happiness;
2. Paradise or heaven;

The Collins dictionary adds that bliss can be

3. Not knowing and not wanting to know about unhappy things or possible problems.

So from what we know, bliss can be a state of mind and heart (utter happiness, ecstasy, or intense pleasure); a place (heaven, paradise); or being unaware (cluelessness, innocence).

An example of bliss might be how you feel about something you own, like a dress or suit, your house, your car, power tools—things, not people. Obviously you love your family, but for the sake of illustration, think about something you own that, whenever you see it, wear it, or use it, you like it. It's a positive state of mind. You feel good about it, you feel contented and blissful. My wife has a relatively new car, a nice brand and style. Every now and then, when we drive together (I like my car too, but mine is thirteen years old, so I'm happy with it for different reasons), we often comment something like,

"I really like this car!" Same with the house—"I love this house."

It goes without saying that all of these physical items may begin by getting our attention, but they will always be in need of our continued attention if, say, three years from now we want them to still be pleasing to us. The car needs maintenance, the dress or suit needs dry cleaning, and the house needs new gutters, carpets, roofing, appliances, or furniture to keep it clean, up to date, or fully functional. There is nothing automatic about maintaining or improving something that we like so that it continues to give us a sense of contentment and happiness. If upkeep or improvement is not intentional, things will break down rather than improve.

A marriage that continually improves makes bliss possible. It is how marriage is intended to be. If we pay attention to improving it, we will be content and blissful, and thirty years from now we can say, "I really love this woman!" or "I'm so glad I married my husband!" It is a great feeling to know you made the right choice at the beginning and that your relationship has improved over the years. That's what I want this book to help you achieve.

Let's face it, most people will have a conviction or an opinion about marriage. Their concept may be formed by ideas about societal expectations, personal experiences, or observing the marriages of the others.

Try this: just ask anyone, "Is it possible to live in marital bliss?" See what kind of reaction you get. My guess is that the first reaction will be a slight pause as your friend decides exactly what to say and how to phrase it. It may be followed by, "Yes, but...." and a list of disclaimers or conditions will be voiced and a variety of opinions will follow. We all know what we want; we just need help achieving it.

Although marriage has been a human institution since the beginning of time, sadly it is often misunderstood and sometimes ends up in the trashcan of discarded negative experiences.

## TOOLS WE CAN USE

There is hope, however, and I believe that with a little help, together we can put some tools in our toolbox, which are nothing less than principles and strategies that we can all use to repair or enhance our lives as married couples. We anticipate that bliss will find its way into the mix.

Unfortunately, one cannot claim expertise about marriage. At best we can observe the successes and mistakes of other married couples and draw conclusions about what might or might not work. Frequently couples end up wishing they had known some of these secrets of happiness at a much earlier stage of their lives.

We can learn from others, and wisdom would suggest that we do so. If we are learners for life we can load up our relational toolbox with the tools we will need—habits, clues, secrets, and principles that will help us live together in harmony and maximize our potential as a couple.

If God is who the Bible says he is, a God who wants the very best for us, and if we can learn and implement the secrets of success in marriage, then life should be an awesome experience from beginning to end. Marital bliss is possible "for as long as we both shall live." It is what we anticipate on our wedding day.

## MARRIAGE CAN BE EXCELLENT

Above all, if being married is analogous to our relationship to God through Jesus Christ, then it should be elevated to the peak of human experience. Sadly, for some it is just the opposite. For many it is a disappointment, a daily battle, or drudgery. But it doesn't have to be that way.

This book is a result of a desire on my part to share a few of the insights I have discovered in the years Cynthia and I have been married, which incidentally, is fifty-one years at the time of writing. We started young. I was twenty and Cynthia was nineteen when we married between my junior and senior years in college. In those days, in New York State where we married, the male age of consent was twenty-one, so my parents had to sign for me since I was legally underage. The female only had to be eighteen, so she was good.

## ON-THE-JOB TRAINING WITH HELP FROM MY FRIENDS

Marriage is on-the-job training, so almost all of our insights have emerged either from personal experience or an abundance of input from specialists, trained counselors, or friends who have told their stories and shared their experiences, and we have tried to listen and learn. Some of the principles in this book have significantly changed our lives and our relationship as a married couple, and we are indebted to those who gave input into our lives. We owe them and are motivated to do what we can, perhaps by way of providing a book such as this, to help others find their way.

I have included principles that may seem obvious at first glance, but in their development I have found some to be counterintuitive, countercultural, not politically correct, or simply surprising in their application. I went through this book and counted more than forty such "surprises" that caught my attention and registered in my mind as having one or more of those elements.

I hope there will be for you, as for me, moments when you will say, "Hmm, I never thought of it that way," or "I never realized that." I trust that those "aha" moments will be as valuable to you as they have been for Cynthia and me as a couple as we have looked for ways to make this journey together a pleasant and profitable one.

What is evident is that those who have paid attention and applied the tools that they have received to their own marriage are the ones who thrive. We hope that when you are through reading this book you will have discovered at least one principle (or several, we hope) that will help you improve your relationships. Perfection is not our goal, but improvement and excellence are, and they are achievable.

    For Cynthia and me our fifty-plus married years have been amazing, and we have very few regrets. As the husband I have been blessed with an extraordinary woman to walk alongside me in this journey. Today Cynthia is a marriage therapist who professionally works with couples in marital crisis. Part of our forty years of ministry in Latin America includes the past fifteen years in which we have applied the principles that work in the counseling context to our seminars. Additionally we have gained insight by cross-referencing the experience of thousands while working with larger groups as well as with couples and individuals. Sharing some of our experiences and insights with so many has proven to be immensely rewarding.

## THE WIFE AS A FITTING HELPER

    I like the way the creation account in Genesis 2:18 states it (NLT): "Then the LORD God said, 'It is not good for the man to be alone. I will make a helper who is just right for him.'" I can trust a God who has my "just right" interests at heart!

    Often in our seminars I will state, "The advantage I have of being married to a marriage therapist is that I get free therapy whenever I need it!" Everyone laughs, but Cynthia and I both know that there is a lot of help for us, and for all who will recognize it, if we can accept the wisdom of God in giving us, especially men, a "fitting helper." She may not be a counselor or therapist, but she can often be God's voice speaking to us!

    So as we see, the Bible word translated "helpmeet" means a "fitting helper." We all need help from our friends, and it makes sense that those closest to us, in this case our wife, is intended by a wise God to be his voice amplified to us to help us find our way in this marriage experience.

This is a how-to book: How to prepare so that your marriage can arrive at the blissful stage and thrive to the end. We will outline ways you can bridge the gap to your spouse on your way to success as a couple.

First, however, let's set the table for this. Marriage, like love, is a many-splendored thing, so no one description captures it all. Also, it is vital to understand what marriage is not. Unfortunately stereotypes and myths clutter the picture of what an ideal marriage should look like.

## WHAT MARRIAGE IS NOT

What is marriage *not*? I admit to being aggravated when I hear someone refer to marriage as a "ball and chain," or the "end of my freedom," or any of a number of putdowns regarding marriage. It would be like buying a new car, never getting it out of first gear because you don't know how the gears work, then griping about the lousy car you bought when in fact you don't know what you are doing. Or buying a new cell phone or camera but never watching a tutorial or consulting an expert and then throwing the cell phone or camera away because "it doesn't work right."

What? That's immature, childish thinking! No, no, no. Time to grow up and put away such erroneous ideas. No one comes into marriage knowing everything. Most of us know very, very little. It is classic on-the-job training!

## THE DNA OF MARRIAGE

## Marriage Is an Adventure

Without question marriage displays high drama, numerous twists and turns, and an abundance of ecstasy (if all goes as it should), sometimes mixed with agony. It is a subject worthy of significant reflection. There are times I wonder, "Did that person have any idea when they started out as a married person that they would be famous some day? Or face serious health threats? Or become a sought-after speaker? Or have to file bankruptcy? Or be crippled in an accident? Or become a millionaire? Or write a #1 hit song or book? Or end up in jail?"

Ask yourselves, "Where will we be twenty-five years from now?" It's the "what if" factor in any life. Some people at an early age have a goal of what they want to achieve. I have met young people who declare that they want to be millionaires before the age of thirty. "You can be anything you want to be," children are told. Yet there are hundreds of variables that impact that future, so no one can guarantee the end result.

What will we have experienced together? Cynthia and I have lived our lives traveling. We have been to seventy-two countries of the world, have met several world leaders, have visited exotic places (we recently flew on a small Buddha Airlines plane around Mount Everest in Nepal), have encountered secluded indigenous tribes in the Amazon jungle, attended huge gatherings of believers in Seoul, Korea, and Sao Paolo, Brazil (a million in each), and visited Maasai tribes while on safari in Africa. Who knew that would happen?

What about the children? Will they grow up to be strong and make one proud? Will they be self-centered and be a heartache? We don't know. Thankfully ours have been a great blessing to us.

*The Seasons of Life*

Every human, as we go from infancy to adulthood, goes through what some have called "the seasons of life." These are biological stages of life. We go from being babies, to childhood, adolescence and youth, and then we grow into the adult phase as young adults, marrieds, parents, and grandparents. Each phase presents its own challenges, and each one, if processed properly, has its own distinct reward. The payoff for navigating well each phase is amazing.

In addition to these biological stages of life, we also have times of tremendous adjustment because of major changes and transitions that we may face. What about the baby or child left with only a single mom but without a father figure? Or a teen left all alone because of tragedy or wrong choices? What about affairs, unfaithfulness between spouses that tears the marriage apart? What about divorce and sometimes the resulting remarriage and blended family and the ensuing mega-adjustments? What about the estrangement of parents and children, in-laws, or grandparents? What about the forgotten or uncared-for elderly?

Life can throw a monkey wrench into our circumstances: a job loss, moving to another state, the death of a loved one, failed opportunities, or huge successes that we often do not handle well. "Empty nest" is always a time for major adjustments as young adult children leave home for college, to marry, or to work elsewhere. The list goes on and on, but with each phase of our life, adjustments, sometimes significant ones, must be made.

*Reinventing Ourselves*

The key ingredient here is that at each new phase, a person must respond wisely to the new circumstances. I use the phrase "reinventing ourselves" to describe the need to adapt to a new reality in our lives. At one time or another, most of us must reinvent ourselves.

For example, when my wife and I moved to our church denomination's headquarters city, Cynthia, who had traveled and participated extensively in our pastoral and overseas ministry, was now home alone. I had been given new administrative responsibilities that required significant travel over my assigned international region (Latin America and the Caribbean), but Cynthia could not always accompany me so what did she do? She reinvented herself—she went back to school to finish her education.

The irony is that she had dropped out of college to marry me, then went back to that same school and graduated thirty-four years later! She finished her Bachelor of Arts in Bible, became an ordained minister, then completed her Master of Arts in counseling, and did three thousand supervised hours of counseling to achieve Licensed Professional Counselor status in the state of Missouri. As it turned out, she connected with a relatively new (at that time) counseling opportunity at National Institute of Marriage, which merged with Focus on the Family and is now Focus Marriage Institute (FMI). FMI is a top-tier entity with an 81% restoration rate for couples that were looking to restore hope in their marriage. Who knew? How do you plan for that?

In the classroom Cynthia discovered that she really loves to study and has been on a learning binge for more than eighteen years as a result, both to her benefit, to mine, and to that of others! Who knew?

The need to reinvent ourselves may come with the birth of a child, a new job opportunity, the empty nest when our kids grow up and leave home, aging parents, or when the loss of a job demands a significant readjustment. Other unforeseen challenges, like the loss of a loved one, a marriage breakup, an unforeseen calamity or disease, abusive behavior by a spouse or other family member, obligate us to make mid-course corrections. We have to adapt to a new reality.

The good news is that for each such transition in our lives, there are steps proven to help us adjust to our next phase of life. However, it is much easier if we have already put in place the safeguards that will hold us solidly together even before the storms of life come and the winds blow.

*Reflecting on the Adventure*

- Ask yourself, "As a couple will we be going strong years from now, or will we have given up on our marriage?"

Separation and divorce are becoming epidemic. It has become easier, much like switching channels on the television, to say, "If this doesn't work, I'll switch to someone else and start all over." One conclusion I have reached is that many couples don't seem to know how to repair their marriages, so they give up, wipe the slate clean, and start over hoping for better results. Most of the time they carry all their old baggage with them into their new marital reality and distort that one as well. They don't know that there are answers that are not that hard to access that will give their marriage what they are really wanting.

- Another question to ask is, "Will we have a family and how will they be raised?"

One counselor said, "Our job as parents is to help our children learn how to be adults even while they are young." It is patently obvious that parents have an enormous influence on their children. One of the most pleasing elements of maturing as parents and grandparents is seeing children and grandchildren grow to be mature and successful human beings. Notwithstanding, there is no guarantee of success for any child because of that x-factor of the choices they make.

- We may also wonder what happy times will we experience and what will have satisfied us?

One of the real satisfactions of being together for several decades, or simply maturing a few years, comes if we have lived in such a way that those who follow admire or even imitate us. That can be quite rewarding if we have had exciting or stimulating life experiences on which we can reflect. Some talk of "living on memories" as a bad thing. We prefer to see them as those accumulated experiences deposited in our memory bank, stored there to carry and stimulate us through the maturing process. Truthfully, I'd rather live with fond memories and happy thoughts of what we've experienced than with the regret, pain, and sadness that often define so many lives. It is rewarding when children and grandchildren love the adventure of creating memories as they travel on their own life journey.

As a pastor and minister, I have had numerous occasions to officiate at both weddings and funerals. Both are fascinating. In my last pastorate in Oregon, a family who had no church affiliation but needed someone to officiate at their father's funeral approached me. Since I did not know the deceased or his family, I did what usually works for me—I interviewed the family members to attempt to get some idea of what this father's life represented to them. It was tough. He had been an alcoholic, couldn't or wouldn't work much, and was generally a disappointment to the family, and, in all likelihood, to himself as well before passing on. It was a huge challenge for me to come up with something that I could use to paint at least some bright colors into his life story.

One of the sons—the siblings were all adults—looked me square in the eyes and said something I have never forgotten: "Preacher, we don't want you to lie about our father!" His message was clear: be straight up about him; we all know the drunken father that he was, so don't paint a false picture of him as some kind of nice guy. I knew exactly what he was saying. I asked more questions, and finally, one of the siblings said, "I remember when we were moving out here to Oregon from the Midwest. We were just kids, but we begged dad to buy us something, and he did. He bought us all some Chiclets!" I saw a tiny smile creep onto their faces as they all relived that small, almost insignificant memory of a moment of happiness they could connect to their dad and to their childhood. I was able to weave a vignette around that one little moment in their lives that had lodged in their collective memories. Chewing gum brought a smile.

It is poignantly sad when a gift of a piece of chewing gum is all there is to tell about a person's life when so much more could have been shared. What will our family remember about us?

- Ultimately we must ask ourselves, how will God view what he has "joined together" as the years pass?

Will he be pleased or disappointed? God is very concerned about every couple, every marriage. It is our hope that some of the things we pass along to you by way of helps for your marriage will bring you to a place where God himself will give his own "well done" stamp of approval on you both. You have met the challenges of life, marriage, and family with honor, confidence, and trust.

## Marriage Is a Mystery

The wisest man who ever lived, apart from Jesus Christ, was a king of Israel named Solomon. In the Bible, 1 Kings 4:32 says Solomon was "wiser than all men" and wrote three thousand wise sayings. These sayings are contained for us in Proverbs, Ecclesiastes, and Song of Solomon, three books in the Old Testament that comprise part of the Wisdom Literature (Job and Psalms are the other two). He also composed 1,005 songs. The man had incredible God-given wisdom and talent.

*The "Who Knows?" Factor*

In one of Solomon's books, Ecclesiastes 11:1-6 (KJV) we find a fascinating treatise on the unknowns of the human experience. I call it the "Who knows?" factor of life in general.

Though we like to plan, project goals, and construct our lives according to our own choices and ideas, life has too many variables that can't be anticipated. Solomon underscores some of that for us in Ecclesiastes 11. Who knows what calamity will blast us, like a tornado, earthquake, accident, tsunami, hurricane, flood, or life-threatening disease? Who knows what trauma, conflict, or personal obstacles will confront us? How often are people derailed in life because they didn't know or "didn't see it coming"?

Likewise Solomon says, "Who knows God's ways?"—the way of the Spirit, or God's handiwork in the marvels of a baby's conception and growth in the womb and birth. Basic anatomy, biology, and astronomy should teach us that the human species and this planet are exceptional and sometimes even unfathomable.

Solomon also encourages perseverance, as well as an entrepreneurial attitude that I like. He essentially says, don't let the tough times keep you from going for it. Don't become fatalistic and decide "if God wants something, it will happen," when oftentimes he is saying, "When you ask for something from me, believe that you receive it and you will have it." Keep trying, because who knows whether this will work, or that, or both? I like the way Solomon reasoned.

*Maximizing the Possibilities*

We cannot make guarantees, but we *can* take steps to maximize the possibilities of success. That's why we write on the subject of marriage and how to close the distance between us as spouses so that the two of us "become one." We *can* prepare in advance and continually implement what we learn so that we lay a strong foundation for the rest of our lives. Marriage is too important to take a chance and see what happens! It must not be approached with the attitude that "if this doesn't work, I'll just try something else and hope for a better outcome!" Why not put the odds in your favor instead and insure success rather than risk disaster?

## Marriage Is a Challenge

*Ending Well*

The ultimate challenge in life is to end well. The search for significance is almost universal. We want our lives to count for something. Yet one of the most poignant statements I have ever heard is this—"No one ends well by accident; ending well is always intentional." I don't know who first said it, but it is a powerful truth.

The same applies to a marriage. No successful marriage happens by accident. A good marriage happens because two individuals purpose to make that possible. It is always intentional. "But we love each other and that's all that counts," you say. Love may cover a multitude of sins, but it also uncovers a multitude of secrets to success. True love invests in the success of the couple. That's where intentionality comes in.

*Being Unequally Yoked*

In the challenge that married life presents, the spiritual component cannot be overlooked. Both the husband and wife must be on the same wavelength spiritually. That is why it is commanded in the Bible that a believing man or woman "be not unequally yoked together with unbelievers" (2 Corinthians 6:14, KJV). A horse and an ox don't plow together; no farmer would harness or join them in the same yoke. They are different in endurance capacity, strength, speed, and temperament. In other words, a believer should not marry an unbeliever. They are individually on different wavelengths and thereby incompatible spiritually. The Bible is clear that the natural (unbelieving) person does not understand the things of the Spirit and in fact cannot comprehend them because they are spiritually discerned (1 Corinthians 2:1, KJV).

For example, there are radio, television, and Internet signals all around us as we read this book, but to see or hear them, we need some kind of receiver to access them. The unbeliever does not have that spiritual antenna or receiver inside, though it is available to him or her if they accept the eternal life God offers them. Without a receiver there is no reception. For instance, you may have a cellphone, but without having a log-on-anywhere plan or knowing the password to access the server, you won't have reception for your phone.

In Ephesians 5:31-32 (KJV) where it speaks of the reason or cause for which a man "leaves his father and mother and is joined unto his wife, and they two shall be one flesh," it follows with "this is a great mystery: but I speak concerning Christ and the church." The obvious analogy is that all believers in Jesus Christ become part of his family. There are about a dozen words in the Bible that describe our relationship to the family of God. All believers collectively comprise the Bride of Christ, which properly understood anticipates our relationship to Jesus Christ in eternity, for which we are being prepared now. Spiritually we are family.

The marriage relationship here on earth is an apt analogy. The "one flesh" principle that applies means that two people, man and woman, become *united* in holy matrimony, not just by a ceremony or the proclamation of a religious official and the governing legal entities, but in a physical (sexual), emotional, intellectual, and spiritual way that bonds them, uniting and closing the distance between them. These aspects will be part of our discussion in this book.

*What Obstacles Do We Face?*

It is possible to live happily ever after, but it is not easy. Why? Because:

- There are practices to learn and tools to discover and utilize. The question, therefore, is, how do we make this relationship work?
- There are hurdles to overcome and enemies to conquer. The question here is, what stands in our way to a successful marriage?
- There are objectives to gain and goals to achieve. Questions: Where do we want to go with this? What is the end game? When we are retirement age, what will we hope to have accomplished?
- There are pleasures and successes to realize, and the question is, what is the payoff for us? And by the way, are we having any fun?
- Ultimately there is a legacy to pass on, and we must ask the question, what good do we leave behind? If our lives should end now, for what will we be remembered? What will they say at our funeral? What epitaphs will be written about us? Did we give up, just survive, or did we thrive? Are we an example to be imitated or to be avoided?

In a personal anecdote, my wife and I were working on a project in Buenos Aires, Argentina, when I was asked to speak at a Bible school there, whose director is a close friend of ours. After being introduced, I made a few opening remarks and introduced my wife, commenting that we had celebrated our fiftieth anniversary the previous summer. The 250 or so young students clapped and cheered, and spontaneously some of the guys jumped to their feet and began to chant loudly, "Sí se puede, sí se puede!" which translated means "Yes, it's possible, yes, it's possible!"

That simple declaration of "yes, it's possible" to stay married for a lifetime made the morning memorable for us. I thought, if nothing else it may be that the idea of an "until death do us part" marriage lodged in some minds and hearts, and who knows how that might help? Maybe that will become a small but important legacy we pass on.

## Marriage Is a Cause

The Scriptures say, "For this cause shall a man leave his father and mother and unite with his wife." I'm going to take liberties with the word *cause* here because it is abundantly clear in practice that marriage as an institution is under fire and has become a cause to fight for!

Without question the modern-day defense of biblical marriage is on center stage. These are some of the issues being debated:

*Just a Man and a Woman?*

Can gays and lesbians be legitimately "married"? Huge debates rage on this one.

*Faithful to One Spouse Only?*

Is the concept of faithfulness to one's spouse relevant today? Or is it an antiquated idea? Is monogamy still in vogue? With infidelity, affairs, wife/husband swapping, swinging lifestyles, living together outside of marriage, and a much higher tolerance for experimentation, it seems like those are in the minority who believe it is always correct to remain sexually and emotionally faithful to one partner. My wife, Cynthia, has observed that although infidelity may be more tolerated in the wider culture, every couple she sees in therapy in which an affair brings them to counseling, the offended spouse never expected it to happen in their marriage. Knowing that many others are being unfaithful does not soften the pain and hurt that one feels. The majority still expects faithfulness.

*Is Cheating on the Rise?*

Several years ago an Internet site that promotes "confidential" affairs for married individuals who want secretly to have "a little fun in their lives" (their motto is, "Life is short; have an affair")[1] blew up when it was revealed that the supposedly confidential information of subscribers had been hacked and was going to be made public for all to see. That meant that thirty-seven million subscribers were in jeopardy of their secrets being shouted from the housetops! Needless to say, it sent shockwaves worldwide.

At the time I thought, "Well, that will sink their ship!" Disturbingly enough, the membership for this hookup site for cheating spouses is now up over fifty million, even after hundreds of thousands dropped out because of the scandal. And according to their own surveys, the site declares, "Regardless of the pain cheating causes, it continues to be on the rise with little signs of slowing down any time soon."[2]

Let's take it one step further. As reported by Taryn Hillin in an article in The Huffington Post, a new survey conducted by this same previously mentioned dating website for people already in relationships sought to discover the link between religion and infidelity by asking 105,000 of its members around the world about their religious affiliation. More than 60,000 of the respondents were in the United States.[3]

As it turns out, one in four members (25.1%) who responded described themselves as "born again" evangelical Christians. Catholics comprised the next largest group at 22.75%, followed by Protestants (22.7%).[4] How can a born-again believer condone or not repent of adultery? Is it because, as Dr. Eric Anderson, a sociologist at the University of Winchester in England, puts it: "People who have faith often use it as an outlet for forgiveness so they're more likely to cheat and less likely to feel guilty"?[5]

Shall we cheat so that we can be forgiven? Shall we sin that grace may abound? It is difficult to comprehend. Faithfulness in marriage is an important cause and one that deserves advocacy.

*What about Divorce and Remarriage Issues?*

Is divorce permissible, and if so, under what circumstances? What about remarriage? Shaunti Feldhahn, a Harvard-trained researcher (Harvard's Kennedy School of Government) has written an excellent book, *The Good News about Marriage: Debunking Discouraging Myths about Marriage and Divorce,* in which she dispels some myths about the divorce rate in the United States.

One of these statistics that has been batted around for years from public speaker to author to reader is that the US divorce rate is about 50%. Feldhahn debunks that statistic saying, "The actual divorce rate has never gotten close to 50%."[6] While doggedly researching the truth about that statistic, she and her team discovered that every well-known speaker or writer whom they interviewed each claimed they had gotten it from someone else, but few recalled from whom.

After her team researched the matter for about eight years, the discovery surfaced: back in the 1970s and early 1980s, the trajectory indeed was showing a significant upward trend of divorce in the US, and people concluded (who knows who was the first) that "if this trend continues, by the year [X], the divorce rate will be 50%."

There it was. People took it and ran with it as fact and not just a projection. Everyone stated it as a given. The reality was that several social and cultural factors kicked in and the first-time divorce rate slowed significantly.

For the record, the percentage of first-time divorces peaked at 40% in 1980 and has declined to about 36% today. While there are many factors that affect that statistic, like couples cohabiting but not marrying, marrying at an older age, or earning a college education, the fact is that for a very long time the higher 50% held up as a "reliable" statistic. It was not; it was in fact a myth. While divorce will always be a serious issue, real numbers serve better than projections or probabilities.

*Is Cohabitation Acceptable?*

On an important and rather sobering side note and keying on the concept of couples cohabiting, living together but not married, the US Department of Health and Human Services interviewed 12,279 women in the US between the ages of 15 to 44 in a National Survey of Family Growth to determine the percentage of women cohabiting with a male partner as a first union. The survey, taken from 2006 to 2010, showed that nearly half (48%) of the women cohabited before marriage, compared with 34% of women in 1995 and 43% in 2002.[7]

Considering that this survey is now more than a decade old, it is possible (careful with probabilities!) that the percentages have increased, though we will not know until further surveys are done. In any case this one fact alone seriously affects any discussion of marriage issues.

Do I detect a pattern? First, have sex before marrying, then try moving in and living with someone, then go for marriage, and if that doesn't work, have an affair, or divorce and get another partner, or sleep around, or . . . well, you get the picture. Society today may be playing by a different set of rules.

The Institute for Family Studies discussed research on cohabitation released by the Center for Disease Control's National Center for Health Statistics, with this conclusion: "Cohabitation has greatly increased in large measure because, while people are delaying marriage to ever greater ages, they are not delaying sex, living together, or childbearing."[8]

That sums it up and appears to underscore the different set of rules I referred to, rules adopted today by many in our culture. It seems that the "friends with benefits" idea is prevalent. You and I need to answer the question, is there a better way? Are there guidelines that will maximize our potential of being happily married? I believe there are.

*Is There a Workable Model for Order in the Home?*

This is a key issue revolving around concepts of authority levels in the home, submission issues, male/female roles and responsibilities, and mutuality. Particularly in religious circles these are hot buttons that can detonate strong feelings.

**Notes**
1. Ashley Madison, Ruby Life Inc., 2001-2019, official website.
2. Paul Tyson. "Study Shows More People Will Be Cheating in 2018," *Kaboom*, January 9, 2018, https://Kaboom-magazine.com/2018/01/09/95950/.
3. Taryn Hillin, "How Many Born-Again Christians Use Ashley Madison," August 12, 2014, https://www.huffpost.com/entry/infidelity-and-religion_n_5447526.
4. Hillin.
5. Hillin.
6. Shaunti Feldhahn, *The Good News about Marriage: Debunking Discouraging Myths about Marriage and Divorce* (Colorado Springs, CO: Multnomah, 2014).
7. Casey E. Copen, Kimberly Daniels, and William D. Mosher, "First Premarital Cohabitation in the United States: 2006-2010," National Survey of Family Growth, *National Health Statistics Reports*, https://www.cdc.gov/nchs/data/nhsr/nhsr064.pdf.
8. Scott M. Stanley and Galena Rhoades, "Why Moving in Together Is So Risky," *Psychology Today*, July 10, 2018, https://www.psychologytoday.com/us/blog/sliding-vs-deciding/201807/why-moving-in-together-is-so-risky.

## Chapter Two:

## A Scriptural Model for a Healthy Marriage

THE TOP-DOWN MODEL: A VERTICAL VIEW

In many of today's cultures the most common model or order (how the home and marriage are structured) is hierarchal. Many see marriage and the family as top-down, with the male being the president and the wife being vice president or more subordinate. The hierarchal view of marriage is often bolstered by an appeal to Holy Scripture, the "natural order" of things, or cultural norms.

**King of the Mountain**

Sometimes I describe this more traditional perspective as my "King of the Mountain" point of view. Additionally, the fact is that I am a big-picture person, which has helped me in my administrative roles in my past work and ministry, but I am not so much a detail person. However, this view has hindered me in the details of relationships and teamwork. So take a cosmopolitan viewpoint and add a moralistic, right-versus-wrong formation, reinforced by the idea that "this is the way things are supposed to be" and that God ordered them to be that way and we—I—have an issue.

As I examined these personal inclinations and thinking patterns, I realized that I automatically assumed and adopted certain reason and logic about my role in the order of things. For my own purposes I look at my way of thinking as one of male privilege, the idea that certain things were within my prerogative to decide. Examples might be which program or channel to watch on television, where we will spend our vacation, who will do the chores around the house, who drives the car when the two of us are going somewhere, what can I spend without consulting my wife, what she can or cannot spend, or who has the final word regarding any family issue.

Reviewing these thought processes, I realized that I had absorbed a rather widespread view that can only be described as one of male entitlement, the notion that as a male, I am entitled to have the last word on any subject. I don't say it, but my brain is hardwired to believe that I do have that right.

In addition, my personal inclination comes from a moralist viewpoint, that is, "my way is the right way and is the better way of doing things." It leads to a sense of moral superiority that is hard to compete with. The key word there is "better."

## It's Tradition!

A few decades ago a popular musical called *Fiddler on the Roof*, produced by Jerry Bock, made the rounds. It was the longest-running musical on Broadway for ten years, and in 2007 *Time* magazine ranked *Fiddler on the Roof* as the seventh most frequently produced musical in American high schools.[1]

The plot centers on Tevye, the father of five daughters, and his attempts to maintain his Jewish religious and cultural traditions as outside influences encroach upon the lives of his family members. We saw a live performance of it in Pompano Beach, Florida, and I cannot forget the intriguing words of the song "Tradition!" written for the musical by Sheldon Harnick in 1964, which gives an insightful view of Jewish culture:

[TEVYE & PAPAS]
>Who, day and night, must scramble for a living,
>Feed a wife and children, say his daily prayers?
>And who has the right, as master of the house,
>To have the final word at home?
>The papa, the papa! Tradition.
>The papa, the papa! Tradition.

There it is in context: "Who has the right, as master of the house, to have the final word at home? The papa, the papa...." I suspect that for many, this is the view that prevails. It's tradition.

## The Divine Right of Kings

Speaking of kings, a historical perspective that inclines strongly toward this view of male privilege or superiority can find its roots in the medieval concept of the divine right of kings, a few of the basic concepts of which are as follows:

1. In every kingdom, the king's power comes directly from God, to whom the ruler is accountable; power does not come to the king from the people, and he is not accountable to them.
2. In every kingdom, the king makes the final decisions on all aspects of government, including the church. Other people and institutions that exercise political power do so as delegates of the king and are subordinate to him.
3. However tyrannically kings act, they are never to be actively resisted (the doctrine of non-resistance). If the king orders an act directly against God's commands, the subject should disobey but must submissively accept any

penalty of disobedience (the doctrine of passive obedience). The doctrine was neatly encapsulated in the satirical song, "The Vicar of Bray," which insisted that "Kings are by God appointed, /And damned are they that dare resist, / Or touch the Lord's anointed."[2]

Thus the king was portrayed as
The figure of God's majesty,
His captain, steward, deputy-elect,
Anointed, crowned...*Richard II*, 4.1

The roots of the concept of male entitlement or privilege and its expressions in divine right, chauvinism, machismo, domestic abuse, master of the house, or male privilege go very deep.

## THE EGALITARIAN MODEL: A HORIZONTAL VIEW

### Equally Yoked: Marriage on a Level Playing Field

A year or two ago, I ran across a published article or dissertation written by Dennis J. Preato, author of various articles on gender issues. Since his conclusions resonate with my knowledge of the Scriptures and my observations of some of the cultural issues and the polemic that surrounds them, the article got my attention. Let me share some of Preato's observations here.

The presentation was titled "Empirical Data in Support of Egalitarian Marriages, and a Fresh Perspective on Submission and Authority" and was presented at an Evangelical Theological Society meeting on April 23, 2004, under the title "Empirical Data in Support of Egalitarian Marriages: A Theological Response."[3]

Preato begins his dissertation with the following assertion: "There is a serious problem with the institution of marriage in the USA. Many marriages, and particularly Christian marriages, don't seem to last. They fall short of God's ideal that marriage should be permanent as long as the two partners live."[4] He then cites a 2001 national study by Barna Research Group that underscores this reality, with Preato and Barna extracting the following:

- According to Barna, 33% of born-again adult Christians have experienced a divorce, which is comparable to non-born-again adults.

- "More than 90% of the born again adults who have been divorced experienced that divorce <u>after</u> they accepted Christ, not before." According to Barna, "that raises questions regarding the effectiveness of how churches minister to families…and challenges the idea that churches provide truly practical and life-changing support for marriage."

- Therapist Dr. Roy Austin agrees with Barna's findings and adds, "Problems occur when some men, as head of the household, become cruel dictators who 'expect their wives to become servants.'"

- By religion Jewish and born-again Christians have the highest divorce rates at 30% and 27% respectively, while surprisingly, atheists and agnostics have the lowest incidence of divorce at 21%. How can this be? Should we all be atheists or agnostics? Of course not. Is it because in the atheist or agnostic worldview, men and women are equally responsible for the health of their marriage? Or is it, as Ron Barrier, a spokesperson for the American Atheists organization, believes, that "there is no room in their ethics for the type of 'submissive' [view] preached by...Christian and/or Jewish groups." Atheists therefore reject the traditional, hierarchal model as "primitive and patriarchal."[5]

**The Elephant in the Room:**
**Why Doesn't the Traditional Model Work?**

In Preato's dissertation he presents what he believes to be the more viable biblical view of marriage, an egalitarian one with both spouses being joint heirs of the grace of God. In it he asks and then answers the intruding question, the elephant in the room: If believers have eternal life and are committed to the Holy Scriptures as the authoritative rule of faith and conduct, then why aren't their marriages working out better than they are? What's wrong with this picture?

I think every believer should ask and then attempt to answer that question. If this is God's way, why isn't it working? Is it possible that our cultural predisposition filters how we interpret the Scriptures? Or are we trapped in the world's mode? What are we missing? Let's look more closely.

# IS THERE CLEAR BIBLE TEACHING ON THE SUBJECT?

**It All Began in the Garden of Eden**

Let's start at the beginning, in the Garden of Eden, where inequality and domination issues have their origins. If any place should have been blissful, it should have been the Garden of Eden!

The issue of inequality of men and women and male domination of the female—or vice versa—is not a new subject. In the Garden of Eden, in what some have described as the "first gender wars," God, speaking to Eve, predicts "you will desire to control your husband, but he will rule over you" (Genesis 3:16, NLT). While this is admittedly a complex and much-debated verse, the concept still holds that when sin entered the world, relationships were distorted until the coming of the kingdom of God in Christ.

Compare this verse with the next chapter where God says to Cain, "Why are you angry, and why has your face fallen? If you do well, will you not be accepted? And if you do not do well, sin is crouching at the door. Its desire is contrary to you, but you must rule over it" (Genesis 4:6-7, ESV).

If we carefully investigate the meaning of the two verses, which both emphasize the words *desire* and *rule*, we see where the clash is: the woman desires to rule over the man, and the man wants to rule over her. Bam! Gender wars. God wasn't saying, "This is the way it is supposed to be," but rather, "it's the way you will want it to be." It was predictive, not prescriptive. Sin messed things up! So the subjection, domination, and submission issue is skewed and distorted because of sin.

## The New Testament View

In Jesus Christ marriage is a new covenant relationship where each spouse is of equal worth, is to be honored and esteemed by all, and is intended to be for life.

Both Malachi, the last book of the Old Testament, and Matthew, the first book of the New Testament, speak of marriage as a covenant intended to be for life.

Marriage is to be highly esteemed and is honorable in all. Since the creation divorce has never been God's intention for couples. He "hates divorce" (Malachi 2:16, MSG) but permits it as an exception to the rule because of mankind's hardened heart. How is divorce problematic?

- Divorce breaks the marriage covenant.
- Divorce may have other painful causes, such as infidelity, abuse, abandonment, or fraud. Neither deception nor violence is biblically permissible.
- Divorce has legal ramifications, with rights, demands, and obligations outlined in almost every culture or country's legal and judicial systems.
- Divorce takes a high emotional and behavioral toll. Acrimony and hatred tend to surface between the couple and spill over onto the children, who are caught in the middle between parents.
- Divorce takes a monetary toll in divided assets, alimony, and legal fees.

Since Jesus Christ came into the world, the new order for humankind has been based on the equal worth of every individual, though not sameness or similarity. In God's eyes, since we bear his image (called *imago Dei*), we are all equal and worthy of dignity before him. First Corinthians 11:11-12 (NIV) captures the idea well: "Nevertheless, in the Lord the woman is not independent of man, nor is man independent of woman. So as woman came from man, so also man is born of woman. But everything comes from God."

There it is, uniqueness on one hand, equality on the other, and God as the source of all. Remember, not identical but of equal value. The whole order of things changes "in Christ."

## Philemon, from Slavery to Brotherhood

As a great illustration of this concept, look at Philemon, a one-chapter book in the New Testament that deals with the relationship between Philemon, a slave master, and his runaway slave, Onesimus. It is estimated that at that time, perhaps one-third of the population of the Roman Empire was slaves.

The apostle who wrote this short letter says in Philemon 15-17 (NIV): "Perhaps the reason he [the runaway slave] was separated from you for a little while was that you might have him back forever—no longer as a slave, but better than a slave, as a dear brother. He is very dear to me but even dearer to you, both as a fellow man and as a brother in the Lord. So if you consider me a partner, welcome him as you would welcome me." In other words, Onesimus was not to be treated as a subordinate but as an equal, a "dear brother."

Better than a slave—as a dear brother, a fellow man, and a partner. It was a new way of treating others as we would want to be treated. Still master and still slave, but now "dear brothers."

In fact, according to Orthodox tradition, Onesimus, who was called Onesimus of Byzantium and the Holy Apostle Onesimus in some Eastern Orthodox churches, was probably this slave to Philemon of Colossae. In a simple but powerful declaration, it is said that Onesimus "went from slave to brother to bishop."[6] In the family of God, one can go from servitude to brotherhood to leadership! Likewise my wife is not my slave or subordinate, but my dear sister in Christ and a joint heir of the grace of God.

We should hope that this concept of equal worth in Christ would prevail in every society, culture, and nation worldwide.

Maybe it is time to declare a "better than a slave" view of wives or husbands and say, "In Christ we are dear brothers and sisters." Therefore a husband and wife are not to treat each other as possessions or subordinates, nor should either exert authority except by mutual consent (1 Corinthians 7:4-5, NIV), but each should treat the other as a spiritual brother and sister, submitting themselves to one another (Ephesians 5:21, NIV).

## Jesus on Domination and Submission

Jesus called his disciples together and said, "You know that the rulers of the Gentiles lord it over them, and their high officials exercise authority over them. Not so with you. Instead, whoever wants to become great among you must be your servant, and whoever wants to be first must be your slave— just as the Son of Man did not come to be served, but to serve, and to give his life as a ransom for many" (Matthew 20:25-28, NIV). We are reminded of what Jesus said regarding divorce—God permits it, but he hates divorce and permits it only because of the hardness of heart. He made it clear that it was not this way from the beginning.

Subjugating the other person as we humans have always done because of hardened hearts is not the way it should be. Thankfully Jesus Christ came to show the world a better way.

The worth of every human being is one of the oldest and most debated cultural seesaws ever encountered by people of every society and nation. Jesus was constantly slandered and derided for his compassion for and loving treatment of women and children. He was a radical because he believed that every human being, man or woman, boy or girl, had equal value in his Father's eyes.

A promiscuous Samaritan woman at a well, the woman caught in adultery, Mary Magdalene, out of whom he cast seven demons, the woman who washed his feet with her tears and anointed him with costly fragrances—all were "sinners," especially in the eyes of the religious and hypocritical leaders of that day. They would say things like, "Doesn't he know what kind of sinner this woman is?" But Jesus lifted these women, restored and affirmed them, and included them in the family of God.

## Insights by New Testament Writers

- "There is neither Jew nor Gentile, neither slave nor free, nor is there male and female, for you are all one in Christ Jesus" (Galatians 3:28, NIV).

- "Wives, submit yourselves to your own husbands as you do to the Lord. For the husband is the head of the wife as Christ is the head of the church, his body, of which he is the Savior. Now as the church submits to Christ, so also wives should submit to their husbands in everything" (Ephesians 5:22-24, NIV).

- "Husbands, love your wives, just as Christ loved the church and gave himself up for her to make her holy, cleansing her by the washing with water through the word, and to present her to himself as a radiant church, without stain or wrinkle or any other blemish, but holy and blameless" (Ephesians 5:25-27, NIV).

- "In this same way, husbands ought to love their wives as their own bodies. He who loves his wife loves himself. After all, no one ever hated their own body, but they feed and care for their body, just as Christ does the church—for we are members of his body. 'For this reason a man will leave his father and mother and be united to his wife, and the two will become one flesh.' This is a profound mystery—but I am talking about Christ and the Church. However, each one of you also must love his wife as he loves himself, and the wife must respect her husband" (Ephesians 5:28-33, NIV).

The man loves his wife like Jesus loves the church, laying down his life for her, and loves her like the man loves himself and takes care of himself. The wife respects and honors her loving, giving husband like she loves Jesus and yields to his love for her. In this way they both submit themselves one to the other.

## When Submission Goes the Second Mile

In my estimation Preato correctly assesses the crux of the matter and what makes submission issues so sticky: if we see our relationship to others, particularly our spouse, as a vertical one rather than a horizontal one, then figuring out how to make that work can be most difficult. However, "Submit yourselves one to another" (Ephesians 5:21, NIV) applies mutually to all of us, not just to "subordinates."

Additionally, as we see in the context of the verse, submitting ourselves to one another is a direct outflow of being filled with the Spirit, along with two other strong characteristics, that is, joy (singing, making music in your hearts) and giving thanks to God for everything. The Spirit-filled person is joyful, grateful, and submissively respectful of others.

Finally, it is easy to think of the word *submission* as having only one meaning or application: "be subject to." That is often the translation given for the Greek word *hupotasso* in numerous scriptural contexts.

However, Preato points out that *hupotasso* actually has two uses: military and non-military. The military has a connotation of being "subject to" or "to obey" as if you are under someone's command…however, the non-military use means "a voluntary attitude of giving in, cooperating, assuming responsibility, and carrying a burden." In ancient papyri the word commonly meant "to support," "append," or "uphold."[7]

In fact various translations do translate "submit" (*hupotasso*) as "be courteously reverent" in Ephesians 5:21 and "cooperate" in 1 Timothy 2:11 and 1 Timothy 3:4, and authors such as Andrew and Judith Lester prefer the translation as "be supportive of," "tend to the needs of," or "respect the needs and desires of."[8]

This coincides with Jesus' teaching that "If anyone forces you to go one mile [compulsory] go with them two miles [voluntary]" (Matthew 5:41, NIV). The first part refers to what was generally considered to be permissible and the custom of Roman soldiers who could obligate anyone they wished to carry their load for them for one mile. In the second part of the verse, Jesus' way was to "assume responsibility and carry the burden" the second mile. Both were submitting, but for different reasons: one because of obligation and the other willingly.

It makes sense: If we are filled with the Spirit, we will indeed cooperate with, uphold, support, and respect others, not just because it is mandated or expected of us, but because as Spirit-filled people we love them and want to cooperate with and lift them. We want to build them up. Isn't that a better way?

We've seen what Bible history says. Let's look at this issue from an investigative and cultural viewpoint. What does secular history teach us? What do marriage and family therapists, sociologists, authors, philosophers, researchers, and demographers tell us about what a happy (or unhappy, as the case may be) marriage looks like?

## ONE HISTORICAL VIEW BY A SPANIARD

Let's leap forward fifteen centuries from Bible days for the viewpoint of a Spanish writer, Miguel de Cervantes Saavedra (b. September 29, 1547–d. April 23, 1616). Cervantes is widely regarded as the greatest writer in the Spanish language and one of the world's preeminent novelists.

His masterpiece, *Don Quixote*, has been translated into more languages (more than fifty) than any other book except the Bible. According to researchers, numerous editions have been released, and in total, the novel is believed to have sold more than five hundred million copies worldwide.

*Don Quixote* is sometimes considered the first modern novel, a classic of Western literature, and among the best works of fiction ever written. Cervantes' influence on the Spanish language has been so great that the language is often called *la lengua de Cervantes* ("the language of Cervantes"). Cervantes writes [English translation]:

> This [book] is from the wise doctor Huarte de San Juan, said Don Miguel, taking it [from Doña Dorotea's hands] ... [I hold it] in great esteem, although I must also say that I have disagreements on...the treatment he gives to women.
>
> Don Miguel looked for it in the book, found the page and read: "Parents who want to enjoy wise children and who have ability for letters have to ensure that males are born, because females cannot reach deep...."
>
> [At this point Cervantes expresses his disagreement with Huarte.] "This opinion of the master Huarte, I have always believed that he has not sufficiently meditated, as would be the case with a sage," Don Miguel said. "The woman, if she does not grow in wit, is like the tree [withered] because it is not watered, and I have for me that, if we educate the daughters with the same liberality and eagerness with which we try to educate the sons, the government of families and nations would be better off. That is why in our family it has been customary for women to learn to read and write, so that they know how to be free and to fend for themselves."
>
> "I think that's very wise, Don Miguel," Doña Dorotea answered. "My parents did the same with me, and that is why I am no less than my brothers, but that each one of us has the powers that nature gave him

without being mediated or hindered in being a man or a woman."

"[I am happy to hear that]," said Don Miguel, "because in our country it is not very frequent. Among us, as soon as a girl reaches the use of reason, they put her to sewing and embroidering, and if they teach her to read, it is by a miracle... Unfortunately we have made women perpetual children, and without preparing them for anything that is not to have children and to rule the house we have titled them as bearers of the honor of the family, which makes them incapable for public life and keeps them locked up and enslaved, first of the father and then of the husband..."

Don Miguel and Doña Dorotea kept talking about the state of women in the different lands Don Miguel knew or had heard about and concluded that the subjection of women was linked to the relative barbarism of each nation.[9]

One more historical note on the subject of the subjection of women is that Cervantes knew firsthand something about servitude, having spent five years as a slave in Algiers in the 1570s, attempting to escape several times.

Gratefully there have been voices over the centuries that have called for a clearer understanding of God's intent for men and women to see each other as God sees us—equal in his sight and bearing his divine image.

## CONTEMPORARY VIEWS ON SUBMISSION AND EQUALITY

What about today? Here are some voices of those who call for us to see each one in the marriage relationship as a joint heir of the grace of God.

Dr. Howard Clinebell, Professor Emeritus of Pastoral Psychology and Counseling, Claremont School of Theology and author of *Basic Types of Pastoral Care and Counseling*, characterizes a healthy marriage as "one evidenced by mutual care and support that allows for the growth and fulfillment of each person's God-given potentialities." Clinebell and his wife, Dr. Charlotte Ellen, add that they can attest to the fact that "egalitarian marriage is potentially more fulfilling for the woman and the man" and that sexism "is a central cause of diminished and destructive marriages."[10]

Drs. Alan Booth and Paul Amato, Penn State sociologists and demographers, agree that egalitarian marriages are happier. They interviewed and followed the lives of two thousand men and women and some of their children over a twenty-year period from 1980 to 2000, personally contacting each six times per year during the twenty-year year study.

After that period, the team of researchers then chose and interviewed a new random sample of 2,100 married couples to be able to "look at two different kinds of changes" that had taken place since the time span of the first study. Dr. Amato comes to this conclusion: "Equality is good for a marriage. It's good for both husbands and wives. If the wife goes from a patriarchal marriage to an egalitarian one, she'll be much happier, much less likely to look for a way out. And in the long run the husbands are happier too."

Dr. David H. Olson, Professor Emeritus, Family Social Science, University of Minnesota, compiled a national survey based on 21,501 married couples using a comprehensive marital assessment tool called ENRICH. This investigative tool represents one of the largest and most comprehensive analyses of marital strengths and stumbling blocks. Couples were asked to complete 30 background questions and 165 specific questions that focused on 20 significant marital issues.

A significant discovery was made in relation to marital satisfaction and role relationships. "It discovered that 81% of egalitarian couples were happily married, while 82% of couples where both spouses perceived their relationship as traditional (hierarchal) were mainly unhappy."

That means only 18% of traditional marriages were reported as happy.

Likewise regarding intimacy, 98% of happy couples feel very close to each other, while only 27% of unhappy couples felt the same. The inability to share leadership equally (couple inflexibility) was the top stumbling block to a happy marriage.

Dr. David H. Olson and Dr. Shuji Asai of the University of Minnesota published a survey on spousal abuse in 2003, again based on sampling of 20,951 married couples taking the ENRICH inventory. The couples with the highest level of satisfaction had the lowest incidence of abuse at 5%, while traditional couple types experienced spousal abuse in 21% of marriages, four times higher than in equality-based marriages!

Dr. Diana Garland, Professor and Chair of the School of Social Work and Director of the Center for Family and Community Ministries at Baylor University, discusses marriage relationships in her book, *Family Ministry: A Comprehensive Guide.* Garland points out that "violence is more likely to occur in homes where the husband has all the power and makes all the decisions than in homes where spouses share decision-making."[11]

Drs. Pepper Schwartz and Philip Blumstein, University of Washington sociologists, published results of a decade-long research study which included an extensive survey of 15,000 American couples which revealed that "equality and shared power significantly contributed to happiness and was the reason couples chose to stay married. Conversely, the inequality experienced by women was a primary cause of unhappiness leading to the breakup of marriages."

Ashton Applewhite, a noted author, addresses the personal and sociopolitical aspects of marriage, citing a 1995 survey of 4,000 women. She notes, "Women in egalitarian marriages are by far the happiest."[12]

Stephanie von Hirschberg, senior editor of the *New Woman Survey*, writes that shared power and responsibility "seem to be crucial to a woman's happiness in marriage."[13]

It appears that a strong case can be made for marriages in which spouses view each other as equals and who esteem and honor each other as the Bible urges us to do.

Conclusion: Over the last fifty-plus years, numerous studies reveal that significant numbers of egalitarian marriages are happy in comparison with traditional hierarchal marriages by an 80% to 20% margin. Maybe it is time to rethink the matter to see if the egalitarian marriage model has a firmer foundation.

ARE BASIC FAMILY VALUES RELEVANT TODAY?

To me it is quite remarkable how values that were taken for granted just a few decades ago are now considered passé and antiquated. Is faith an important component in a marriage or family? How important is kindness? What about humility? Modesty? Generosity? Simplicity? Contentment? Integrity? Love? Faithfulness?

What about intimacy (both physical and emotional) and relational issues? A short list of issues might include abuse, aggression, distancing, disinterest, absenteeism, false or exaggerated expectations or demands, among a host of other issues. We will look at these more in depth as we proceed.

**Notes**
1. Broadway.com Staff, "L'Chaim! 50 Facts about Fiddler on the Roof on the Musical's 50th Anniversary," *Broadway Buzz*, September 22, 2014, https://www.broadway.com/buzz/177572/lchaim-50-facts-about-fiddler-on-the-roof-on-the-musicals-50th-anniversary/.
2. Brian Duignan, "Divine Right of Kings," *Encyclopaedia Britannica*, https://www.britannica.com/topic/divine-right-of-kings (most recent revision).
3. Dennis J. Preato, "Empirical Data in Support of Egalitarian Marriages and a Fresh Perspective on Submission and Authority," God's Word to Women, www.godswordtowomen.org/Preato3.htm.
4. Preato.
5. Preato.
6. "Apostle Onesimus of the Seventy," https://oca.org/saints/lives/2015/02/15/100526-apostle-onesimus-of-the-seventy.
7. Preato.
8. Andrew D. Lester and Judith L. Lester, *It Takes Two: The Joy of Intimate Marriage* (Louisville, KY: Westminster John Knox, 1998), 120.
9. Miguel Cervantes Saavedra. *Don Quixote de la Mancha* (Barcelona: Ediciones Océano).
10. Howard Clinebell, *Basic Types of Pastoral Care and Counseling: Resources for the Ministry of Healing and Growth* (Nashville: Abingdon, 1984), 244-50.
11. Diana R. Garland, *Family Ministry* (Downers Grove, IL: IVP Press, 1999), 200-201.
12. Ashton Applewhite, "Making Relationships Work Better," http://www.divorceonline.com/articles/140953.html, accessed November 7, 2003.
13. Preato.

# Chapter Three:

## Guiding Principles for Connecting to the Right Mate

There are four basic scriptural components fundamental to finding and marrying a mate as referenced by Jesus in Matthew 19:5-6 (NLT): "'This explains why a man leaves his father and mother and is joined to his wife, and the two are united into one.' Since they are no longer two but one, let no one split apart what God has joined together." The four components are:

- Leaving "father and mother" (i.e., the family of origin).

- Cleaving "unto his wife," to be united or joined to or with, sticking or being glued to. Note that to "cleave" has two meanings: "cut," as a butcher's cleaver is for cutting or chopping meat; the opposite meaning is "to adhere to, stick to, or join with." It is a unique joining of two people into one entity.

- Joined, united into one ("[they] shall become one flesh," Matthew 19:5, NIV).

- Inseparable (Let nothing or no one split apart, come between, or separate "what God has joined together" (Matthew 19:6, NIV).

# LEAVING

## Our Comfort (or Discomfort) Zone

First, in the context, "leaving" means leaving home, parents, the family of origin. It's time to leave our comfort zone (in some cases, our discomfort zone) and that to which we are accustomed, our family, and start a new entity or family. What is the goal of the new couple and future father and mother of their family? Jessie Minassian, a popular speaker, blogger, and author of twelve books on family relationships, states: "Our goal as parents is to help our kids reach adulthood before they leave our home, not hope they figure it out after they leave."[1]

## Negative Family Traits

"Leaving" also means not hanging on to your negative family traits, customs, or habits. Some like to take refuge in statements like "that's the way we always celebrate holidays," or "Where I come from drinking alcohol is perfectly acceptable," or "Cussing is not such a big deal. Everyone does it."

Often these are excuses for continuing what we have always seen in action, like saying, "My ancestors were Irish and we get angry, but we get over it!" Leaving our family of origin issues allows us to reexamine who we are and why we do what we do. It is what keeps good counselors in business as they help people evaluate these matters and redirect them to a better, more productive future.

To be clear, we will later refer to family traditions and history as anchors for our own lives, but what we leave behind are the negative or counterproductive and customary behaviors and attitudes that do not contribute to a mature approach to life. Positive traditions are useful; negative traits are to be discarded or modified.

## Abuses and Trauma

"Leaving" also means recognizing and dealing with any abuses or traumas that have been part of our upbringing. The scars of family trauma can affect a person for life, but those scars don't have to be permanent. Interestingly there is that strong "let's start all over again" element to the biblical concept of being "born again" and becoming "a new creature in Christ."

## Defects in Temperament

Another aspect of "leaving" can mean leaving behind the defects in temperament that are a part of our family history, such as the tendency to addictions (alcohol, drugs, gambling), or anger, divorce, sexual promiscuity, sarcasm, depression, abuse, or suicide. These characteristics can explain your past, but they don't have to define your future. You can "leave" them.

## Incorrect Values

"Leaving" can also mean modifying incorrect values that characterize our family. In other words, what is important to your parents may or may not be values you want to share with them. Examples might be a tendency to stinginess or hoarding, overly strict discipline, careless spending, or a sort of "help yourself" attitude that justifies stealing or shoplifting by saying, "They have more than enough; they'll never miss it if I take a little."

Some parents are habitually late, or negative, or manipulative, or liars, or cheaters—and behind such behavior is a value that excuses it ("I deserve my fair share, it doesn't really matter, they'll never miss it, the end justifies the means, whatever it takes to get ahead, she'll never know"). You cannot bring these corrosive attitudes to a new marriage! It's time for a fresh start. It's time to cut the cord on old and valueless habits.

Dennis and Barbara Rainey wrote an insightful article for *Family Life* titled "Respectfully Leaving Your Parents." They begin with this declaration from psychologist Dan Allender in *Intimate Allies*: "The failure to shift loyalty from parents to spouse is a central issue in almost all marital conflict."[2]

## Crippling Dependencies

The Raineys suggest several areas from which one might need to distance themselves, while emphasizing that "leaving father and mother" does not mean abandoning or ignoring them. Here is how they put it: "Leaving your parents does not mean ignoring them or not spending any time with them. Leaving your parents means recognizing that your marriage created a new family and that this new family must be a higher priority than your previous family."[3]

*Emotional Dependency*

For example, one must break away from a potentially disastrous emotional dependency on one's mother or father. In this day of easy Internet access, FaceTime, Skype, and other social media outlets, it can be a temptation to never break away from the emotional bonds that hamper us in establishing a new home and family. Let's face it—it is often easier to talk to parents or siblings nonstop every day, thus inadvertently placing a higher value on that communication than connecting with one's spouse or children.

*Financial Dependency*

It is also important to leave behind our financial dependency on our parents. This does not mean that parents cannot help the newlyweds or the grandchildren in their time of need. It does mean that great care must be taken by both the parents and the children or grandchildren not to abuse that relationship by always taking and never giving back or repaying. This is known as enabling and creates a possibly crippling dependency. The fact is that the day may come when the roles are reversed and the parents who can no longer work or are widowed may find themselves depending on their children. That's why 1 Timothy 5:3-4 (NIV) is so emphatic when it speaks about "those widows who are really in need…but if a widow has children or grandchildren, these should learn first of all to put their religion into practice by caring for their own family and so repaying their parents and grandparents, for this is pleasing to God." That's a clear mandate about the responsibilities of family members to each other.

My mother-in-law immigrated legally to the US from Norway, eventually marrying Arthur, a Swedish illegal immigrant (later granted status through amnesty), and producing two amazing daughters. In their later years, they sold their little cottage on Long Island and made arrangements to designate, upon their passing, half of the proceeds of the sale for each daughter. However, that amount and her hard-earned savings after my father-in-law's passing was in her control until her passing at the age of ninety-five. Cynthia and her sister were always respectful of their mother and never abused the privilege of having access to her mother's funds while helping her manage them, though her mother would probably never have known had they done so.

When she asked our opinion about spending a considerable sum of money for something that wasn't "a necessity", like all new crowns for her teeth, or whatever else, we would tell her, "It's your money, and if you want to spend it all now, that is your choice." We could tell she liked hearing that! It was not our money, and we had no right to "help ourselves to it." We kept our distance from both financial dependency and covetousness when it came to the financial wellbeing of our parents.

*Decision-making Dependency*

Decision-making dependency can be tricky. Beware of constantly looking to mom or dad for their input before making decisions. Seeking wise counsel is good, but "leaving father and mother" implies making decisions between you and your spouse. Decision-making dependency can put you in the awkward position of having to side with either your parents or your spouse, putting them on opposite sides and creating tension. Obviously parents must learn to release their adult children and let them form their own family unit without interference, but at the same time married children must accept the responsibility for making their own decisions as a couple, even while honoring their parents. If married couples do not heed this warning, I can almost guarantee friction and tension, and certainly hard feelings.

*From Dependency to Honor*

"Honor your father and your mother" is one of the Ten Commandments. But how can we cut the ties of dependency without dishonoring our father and mother?

It is interesting that the Bible gives two back-to-back commands to children as it relates to their relationship to their parents. One is, "Children, obey your parents in the Lord, for this is right." The writer, the apostle Paul, follows with a quote from one of the Ten Commandments that Moses gave in Deuteronomy: "Honor your father and your mother, as the Lord your God has commanded you, so that you may live long, and that it may go well with you" (Deuteronomy 5:16, NIV). When the writer quotes this command in the New Testament he adds parenthetically, "which is the first commandment with promise," that is, "that you may live [enjoy] a long life on the earth, and that it may go well with you" (Ephesians 6:2-3, NIV).

While we are children, our responsibility is to obey our parents. Learning to obey those over us begins at an early age. Unless a child learns to respect authority, a spirit of rebellion will often form in that child's heart and mind and the child will usually insist on doing things their way. Learning to submit to others honors them and is the key to a successful life. Even if a child does not have good parents, insofar as it is possible, they should obey them in the Lord. "In the Lord" means if you do your part in obedience and respect for your parents, God will keep his promises to you and "it will go well with you."

"Children, obey your parents." That's fairly simple; adults are certainly more experienced, often are wiser, and their directions should be heeded. The exception, of course, is any demand that directly contradicts God's commands. For example, a parent cannot order a child to commit a sexual act and say they must do so because they are "to obey their parents." In God's eyes this is one of the worst forms of evil, and Jesus himself says such an adult who commits that horror is so evil that he or she deserves to have a heavy weight tied around their neck and be tossed into the sea. That's how God feels about it, and such a person goes on God's condemnation list.

One pastor told of a woman in his congregation who came to him for counseling, and her issue was, "My husband wants me to have a threesome with me, him, and another woman. The Bible says that I should submit to him, so does that mean I should do it?" Of course the answer was no. The Bible clearly teaches that "sin shall not have rule over you," so a wife does not submit herself to sin in that context. To go along with it is to literally break the one-flesh principle and the marriage covenant. Again the Bible is clear. Hebrews 13:4 (NASB) states it, "Marriage is to be held in honor among all, and the marriage bed is to be undefiled; for fornicators and adulterers God will judge."

Hear me clearly: If you are having sex with someone to whom you are not married, you are headed for judgment. Repentance is in order. Cheating on spouses is on the rise, we know, in spite of the consequences but beware— cheating on your spouse, adultery, means you are facing trouble.

After you become an adult, honor your father and your mother. Don't despise, dishonor (how about if we get rid of the tendency once and for all to refer to our parents as "my old man" or "my old lady"), ridicule, or ignore them, but rather keep the communication lines open. Respect them, honor them on special days, and visit them when possible. Be attentive to their needs. As they grow older, God is pleased if we do what we can to help alleviate those needs, especially if they are widowed and become financially or physically dependent.

Positive action toward our parents and in-laws honors God and helps build bridges to our spouse. It reduces tension in the marriage and calms unsettled emotions. We can leave father and mother without dishonoring or ignoring them.

I will confess that I am on a personal campaign to counteract the infamous mother-in-law jokes that seem to be so popular. I understand that many times the parents or especially the mother of the person we marry may have strong feelings about "her baby" or "her boy" getting married.

I also grant that I was blessed with a good mother-in-law who loved God (that was the key) and loved her daughters and who understood that her girls married men who also loved God. She didn't agree with everything, but she made her personal commitment to God to put us firmly in his hands and not meddle. We honored and respected her, and she gave us space to be who we were designed to be. We had very few disagreements as a result.

My mother-in-law was almost ninety-six years old when she passed away. She lived with us the last three years of her life, and truthfully, we were blessed by being able to help her at the end of her time. We still have warm memories of her. She and my father-in-law blessed us; it was right to honor and take care of them. When we repay father and mother by attending to their needs in their old age, it makes God very happy.

## CLEAVING

### Accepting the Harness

As we have seen, cleaving means being joined together, stuck like glue to each other. In rural societies oxen were joined in a yoke so that they could plow together in rhythm with each other without pulling against the other or each one wandering off to do their own thing.

Likewise a horse or a team of horses (when pulling on a stagecoach) had to wear a harness since speed was involved. The harness allowed the driver to guide, slow down, or speed up the horses. The same principle applied to a single horse, and in a sense, the horse and driver are connected for the purpose of achieving the goal of speedy progress.

### War Horse—Born to Run but Taught to Plow

Joyce Williams, director of women's ministry at Christ Center in Cashmere, Washington, wrote a timely article picking up this theme from the movie *War Horse*.

> If you saw the movie *War Horse*, you may remember the scene where a teenage boy had to teach a stallion to plow in order to keep the horse. It was such a hard thing for that horse to carry a heavy, boring burden in the heat and dirt—after all, he was designed to run like the wind.

Years later the stallion was captured in battle. The enemy colonel tells a soldier to make another horse pull a cannon wagon. When that horse rears and fights the harness, the colonel shoots it. He then orders the soldier to make the stallion pull the cart or he will shoot it too. When the soldier approaches, anticipating stamping hooves and a snorting, resistant head, the stallion not only stands still but lowers his head to receive the harness and willingly pulls the cart.

The soldier profoundly observes, "Whoever taught you to pull the plow just saved your life."[4]

Learning to submit to and work with others begins when we are babies. We are not naturally submissive when we are born. Like the stallion, we want to run like the wind, to do things our way. We are born with a "me first" attitude. We resist the harness. When children play, we often hear their favorite word, "Mine!" We were all born self-centered, even selfish.

Many want to be married for the "benefits" but still want to reserve to themselves the right to do their own thing, to act like a single if they wish, to have no accountability to anyone else, to make all decisions on their own. A husband who only wants to hang out with his buddies or a wife who is constantly going out with her girlfriends is creating a vacuum in the marriage. I love to watch men who talk with their wives, play with the kids, respect their role as husband and father, and care for the needs of the family. Wives who love and respect their husband and family above all others are a wellspring of life.

When we learn to lower our head to take the harness instead of rearing up, we set the stage for a much more harmonious marriage and family life. Again the Bible is clear: "Submit yourselves one to another." Let's lower our heads to accept the harness.

The greatest example was Jesus Christ, of whom Philippians 2:6-8 (AMP) says,

> Although He existed in the form and unchanging essence of God [as one with him, possessing the fullness of all the divine attributes—the entire nature of deity], did not regard equality with God a thing to be grasped or asserted [as if he did not already possess it or was afraid of losing it]; but emptied Himself...[giving up the outward expression of divine equality and His rightful dignity] by assuming the form of a bond-servant, and being made in the likeness of men [he became completely human but was without sin, being fully God and fully man].

We can love our spouse and others as Christ loves us, not grasping at his Godhead but giving that up and laying down his life in humility, not insisting "I'm the head, the high priest here, so do as I say." By serving and edifying the other person, loving them as Christ loves his church, we demonstrate the kingdom culture Jesus came to model for us. That's what "esteeming the other better than ourselves" and acting in "lowliness of mind" amounts to. Our model, Jesus Christ, said it best: "But I am among you as one who serves" (Luke 22:27, NIV).

I recall my father telling a story about a married couple where the wife was a faithful believer but where the husband had lapsed into alcoholism and from time to time would come home in a stupor and act like a brute. During one holiday season, the wife had prepared a wonderful meal for the following day. Everything, including a large turkey waiting to be baked in the oven for a few hours, was set to go. The husband came home drunk that night, and he was hungry. He saw the raw turkey that was waiting to be baked the next day, and in his drunkenness, started pulling off chunks of raw turkey and eating it. The next morning when his wife discovered what her drunken husband had done, she calmly went to work salvaging what she could of the meal. One of her friends asked her later how she could remain so "in control" (i.e., lower her head to take the harness), to which she replied, "I don't know what lies in the future for my husband, but this may be the only heaven he will ever know!" She could have done a lot of nasty things. She chose to see the bigger picture instead. She was therefore willing to cleave to her husband even at great personal cost.

The "leave and cleave" in the marriage bond is also a picture of the union God wants us to have with him—leaving your other gods, your past, your false ways, and living by a new allegiance. "You shall walk after the LORD your God, and fear him, and keep his commandments, and obey his voice, and you shall serve him, and cleave unto him" (Deuteronomy 13:4). The NIV translates "cleave unto him" as in "hold fast unto him." Of course that is the whole idea.

In Genesis 2:24, the man leaves his father and mother and clings or cleaves to his wife. In this context to cling or cleave means to be faithfully devoted to, the same as in "Rather, cling tightly to the LORD your God as you have done until now" (Joshua 23:8, NLT). The word *cleave* is an old English word meaning that the husband and wife are to count on each other, share with one another, give their best, and stick together through thick and thin.

When a spouse leaves their previous friends or lovers, they likewise commit to their partner (in the traditional vows, "to love him/her, comfort him/her, honor him/her and keep him/her, in sickness and in health, and forsaking all others keep only unto him/her so long as you both shall live." You leave all others, and you cling to the one.

## JOINED

Marriage is viewed as a lifelong commitment where the two become one flesh. They share an intimate relationship based on devoted love, faithfulness to each other, mutual respect and trust. An intriguing analogy in 1 Corinthians 6:16-17 (NIV) says, "Do you not know that he who unites himself with a prostitute is one with her in body? For it is said, 'The two will become one flesh.' But he who unites himself with the Lord becomes spiritually one with him." So physical intimacy is analogous to spiritual intimacy in this context.

Sex is for married couples by which they unite themselves with one another. Ideally marriage should and can be a delightful sexual adventure for a lifetime. The way the human body is created is evidence that sexual intimacy is more than something designed for procreation. We are also created to delight in the experience of sexual intimacy. Sex for a married couple should be delightful!

However, it is very clear that having any kind of extramarital affair jeopardizes the one-flesh principle designed exclusively for a married couple. Perhaps our culture has trivialized adultery and fornication (sex outside of marriage), so that it is merely a hook-up, a fling, or a casual encounter. Additionally, today's culture sometimes projects the mistaken notion that a married person or couple is permitted to play around as long as it is allowed or suggested by the spouse. In their view it isn't cheating if it is consensual. Some even suggest that "this [extramarital relationship] helps our marriage." Not so.

The Bible is clear. Hebrews 13:4 states it, "Marriage is to be honored by all, and the [marriage] bed undefiled: but fornicators and adulterers God will judge." Hear me clearly—if you are having sex with someone to whom you are not married, danger is pending. Repentance is in order.

Cheating on spouses is on the rise in spite of the consequences, but beware—cheating on your spouse means trouble is ahead.

## INSEPARABLE

Faithfulness in marriage, which in a sense is even more far-reaching than monogamy, is a high value today more than ever. Monogamy means having one spouse; faithfulness means never cheating on that spouse.

I came across this quote by Daniel Bergner, a journalist and contributing editor to the *New York Times Magazine*, in an article about sex drive:

> Monogamy is among our culture's most cherished and entrenched ideals. We may doubt the standard, wondering if it is misguided, and we may fail to uphold it, but still we look to it as to something reassuring and simply right. It defines who we aim to be romantically; it dictates the shape of our families, or at least it dictates our domestic dreams; it molds our beliefs about what it means to be good parents. Monogamy is... part of the crucial stitching that keeps our society together, and that prevents all from unraveling.[5]

How can we become one flesh, united with our spouse physically, emotionally, and spiritually in such a way that it reflects our uniting spiritually with God himself through Jesus Christ? This is the fundamental issue that we are addressing here.

We trust that you actually want to draw closer to each other. There is no escaping the fact that there has to be a "want to" for it to happen. Though some may feel like the "want to" has long since flown out the window, if there is a real desire to close the distance between you and your spouse, there is good news for you.

**Notes**
1. Jessie Minassian, "Four Powerful Ways to Love Your Teens and Help Them Like You Back (Maybe)," *Focus on the Family* (February/March 2018), https://www.focusonthefamily.com/parenting/teens/parent-teen-connection/4-powerful-ways-to-love-your-teens-and-help-them-like-you-back-maybe.
2. Dan Allender, *Intimate Allies* (Carol Stream, IL: Tyndale House, 1999).
3. Dennis Rainey and Barbara Rainey, "Respectfully Leaving Your Parents," *Family Life*, https://www.familylife.com/articles/topics/marriage/getting-married/newlyweds/respectfully-leaving-your-parents/.
4. Joyce Williams, "Pull That Plow!" Facebook blog, May 23, 2014.
5. Daniel Bergner, "What Do Women Want?" *New York Times Magazine*, uploaded by Southern California Public Radio.

## PART TWO

**16 WAYS TO CLOSE THE GAP BETWEEN YOU AND YOUR SPOUSE**

# Chapter Four:

## Affection Wins

In what ways can spouses close the gap to each other? World renowned for his work on marital stability and divorce prediction, Dr. John Gottman has conducted forty years of breakthrough research with thousands of couples. Dr. Gottman has been named one of the Top 10 Most Influential Therapists of the past quarter-century by the Psychotherapy Networker.[1] He is the author or co-author of more than two hundred published academic articles and more than forty books, including the bestselling *The Seven Principles for Making Marriage Work*, *What Makes Love Last*, *The Relationship Cure*, *Why Marriages Succeed or Fail*, and *Raising An Emotionally Intelligent Child*.

Gottman is a professor emeritus of psychology at the University of Washington and heads The Relationship Research Institute and the Gottman Institute with his wife, Dr. Julie Schwartz Gottman. The institute provides therapeutic treatment to couples and trains professionals in the Gottman Method. After decades of research, Gottman has arrived at a startling, yet not unexpected, quality that almost guarantees success in any relationship but especially in marriage: kindness. That's right, kindness.

## # 1. KINDNESS IS THE SUPERPOWER

According to numerous researchers, kindness is a primary component in a successful marriage. Two premier psychologists/analysts, John Gottman and Shaunti Feldhahn, put kindness ahead of all human qualities. In fact, Feldhahn has written a book that has taken off in businesses and enterprises—*The Kindness Challenge: 30 Days to Improve Any Relationship.* Here's what one reviewer writes: "After years of extensive research, Shaunti Feldhahn has concluded that kindness is a superpower. It can change any relationship, make your life easier and better, and transform our culture."[2] I agree that kindness is indeed a superpower.

In my view kindness is almost a guarantee of success in life. In our Youth Congresses, which we still conduct (believe it or not) at our age, we will tell the youth that if they want to be guaranteed success in their lives and careers, learn to be kind. "Be kind one to another, tenderhearted, forgiving one another" (Ephesians 4:32, KJV). Kindness is fundamental to a good life and crucial to a healthy marriage. It is a revolutionary power. Being kind is not always convenient. Life can be tough and even cruel, but a kind spirit will overcome huge obstacles. Ask yourself, am I a kind person?

Sometimes I see kindness even in commercial contexts. I know that sales clerks must be kind and not uppity because that is, or should be, how they attract customers and increase sales. But when an employee, like a shelf stocker at a grocery store, goes out of their way to help, it shows kindness. And it seems to be catching on.

Recently in a supermarket I stopped a worker in one aisle and asked where I could find a certain item. She put down what she was doing and said, "Here, let me show you." She could have said, "Over there, five aisles over" and that would have helped me, but she took me right to the item instead. It was inconvenient for her but helpful to me, the customer. I thanked her for her kindness.

## Kindness Described

Gottman defines kindness as "generosity of spirit," which displays itself in four ways.[3] A person is kind when
- They are distracted, stressed, or fatigued but still act positively toward another;
- They give the benefit of the doubt, not looking so much at consequences but focusing on the intentions of another;
- The two may be arguing but they don't fight dirty or cross the line, saying or doing something that may cause pain that won't be forgotten;
- They share joyful events and happenings. The home should be a safe place to share happy events, like a promotion, getting a compliment, receiving an award, without someone knocking you down because they don't want you to "get proud" or "get a big head." The world beats us up enough. Let's help create a comfort zone where spouses and family members can expect positive affirmation.

To whom else can you brag and be affirmed without criticism? Do you know that some people instinctively douse the flames of happy moments because they have grown up to fear pride so much they fail to affirm good behavior? Couples and families are allowed to brag to each other. She says, "My boss told me today that I am one of his best workers," and he says, "I'm glad he recognized what I've known all along!"

We live in a culture that doesn't like those who brag and tries to pull them down, but there is a difference between bragging, which can often be a silent cry for affirmation, and sharing our joy and being affirmed. Kind words of affirmation are just about the most powerful human motivator there is. We all need it.

Chip and Joanna Gaines had a very successful reality television show in the US called *Fixer Upper* which aired on HGTV from 2013 to 2018. They are also successful authors. On *Fixer Upper*, they remodeled homes for people, and it was always fascinating to see the before and after of their work. What I loved about the show was how Chip and Joanna interacted with each other and with their team, as well as with the couple or family buying the home. I have noted how often Chip or Joanna, in their work talk and repartee, affirmed each other with little comments like, "Yes, I like that idea," or "Good job!"

Sometimes one of them would make a suggestion and I would instantly focus on the response, knowing how easy it is to counter-suggest or discard the idea. Most of the time, they showed their love and respect for the other by affirming the verbalized concept. If they were trying to find a better way, they would negotiate it, but always respectfully and positively. Occasionally four of their five children would be on the show, and Chip and Joanna were the same with them, affirming and respectful of their work and ideas.

Being kind is not that hard to do unless our mindset is negative. Overhauling our view of others, especially of our spouse, will quickly close the distance between us. Putdowns, critiquing, constantly correcting or negating will not build bridges to anyone.

Even in ordinary ways, the affirmation principle works. I have a new dentist whose team is excellent in this matter, and I recently complimented them on it. Throughout the teeth cleaning process, the various dental helpers and technicians said things like, "Excellent" or "Perfect" or "That looks good." They all did it, and I was impressed by how that felt and the atmosphere it created in the dental office.

## Creating a "Yes" Culture

I'm not certain when or how it evolved with us and our three kids, but Cynthia and I had a philosophy of life that included the concept that "the answer is yes unless there's a good reason to say no." Our three kids knew growing up that they would get a yes answer on anything they might aspire to or attempt—unless Mom or Dad knew something they didn't know or had a valid concern. And they could always appeal a "no" from us. It was negotiable. To this day our three have raised or are raising their children, our eight grandchildren, with a "go for it" zest for life.

We weren't perfect in our decision-making, but our kids respected our views as parents, and since they knew the answer would be yes in most cases, they knew the boundaries and were content to accept our guidance.

In our seminars and conferences it is surprising how many attendees confess that they were raised by parents whose default answer was an authoritarian "no". Why? "Because I said so." No other reason.

From where does a yes concept come? Not surprisingly, we find that it is part of God's nature. "If God is for us, who can be against us?" (Romans 8:31, NASB) and "For all the promises of God find their Yes in him" (2 Corinthians 1:20, ESV). Finally, he "richly gives us all things to enjoy" (1 Timothy 6:17, KJV). God's culture for us is a big, affirmative yes!

It's quite disturbing to observe how often we forget the nice, easy kindnesses that would drastically improve a marriage relationship. Kindness seems like a given, but it is easily overlooked.

I like the counter-movements I see from time to time, like people who do, and challenge others to do, random acts of kindness (RAK for short). They do just that—pick someone out, a stranger, and do something nice for them "just because." Likewise there are those who "pay it forward," when someone gives to them and they turn around and bless someone else.

In 2017 my wife and I attended a large conference of Christian counselors in Nashville, Tennessee, and I chose a workshop in which Shaunti Feldhahn was the presenter. She told an amusing account of one woman who attended a similar presentation by Feldhahn, whose book on kindness had just come out, and of course she was emphasizing this "superpower."

Suddenly, one lady attending the workshop jumped up and ran out of the conference. Later she returned and sheepishly approached Feldhahn to explain: "As you were talking, I realized that I had thoughtlessly charged out of the house this morning as I headed for this conference. On my way out the door I remembered passing my husband, who was on a ladder busily fixing something in the entryway to our house. I didn't kiss him goodbye or even say goodbye. I realized how unkind I was, totally ignoring my husband. I had to text him and apologize for being rude. That's why I ran out." She paused, then added, "His text in reply to me was, 'Who are you and what have you done with my wife?'" We all laughed because though humorous, it struck a responsive chord in all of us. How easily we forget to be nice.

Kindness is the most important ingredient in any relationship, but especially in a marriage. The Bible is definitive about it—be kind one to another, tenderhearted, forgiving one another.

**The Power of Saying "Thank You"**

Most of us can almost hear our mother's words lodged in our memory: "What do you say?" Obviously the answer is "Thank you!" In an addendum to the concept of the value of kindness, Feldhahn reveals an intriguing side note, which is the value of saying "thank you" as an expression of kindness: "You don't think 'thank you' matters that much? You couldn't be more wrong! In our surveys, 72% of all men said it deeply pleases them when their wives notice their effort and sincerely thank them for it. Believe it or not, 'Thank you' is manspeak for 'I love you!'"[4]

I think she nailed it. I know how good it feels when Cynthia acknowledges some small thing I do or some chore, something that she could easily take for granted. I get a little buzz of euphoria in my brain. It makes me feel good and shows me that I'm not overlooked, that what I did was important enough for her to affirm. A small thing, but it does say, "I love you."

**Extolling Virtues**

I must add one last expression of kindness—extolling. Though not commonly used, it is a word often found in a context of "extolling the virtues of." It means "praising enthusiastically."

When I hear a husband or wife praising their spouse and telling other people about something their spouse did or some quality they admire in them, it is a powerful experience. That is partly because it is rarer than it should be, plus it has the double impact of not only making the spouse look good, but the person who is speaking is esteemed in our eyes as well.

We had two prominent couples over for dinner recently. One, a published author and well-read minister, commented, "My wife is my favorite theologian!" Although his wife would not classically be regarded as a theologian, both my wife and I find her views about scriptural subjects fascinating. She does have a unique way of seeing truth, and hearing her own husband extol her capacity to see things from a unique perspective was heart-warming to say the least. I came away from that conversation with a loftier view of both of them.

I know that if I overhear Cynthia telling someone else about something nice that I did, I feel euphoric! An added value is that it puts a person in a frame of mind to look for those good qualities in their spouse. It forms positive habits!

## # 2. ROMANCE STOKES THE FIRE

Romance plays such a large role in our premarital relationship. Guys who later claim to not have emotions are all over that girl, wooing and trying to win her with texts, notes, calls, poems, caresses, and a lot of sweet talk. But in some cases the years pass and that same man will turn cold, ignoring his wife and showing no interest in her welfare. Likewise a girl can revel in the romance but after a few years get bogged down in the tedium of life. The spark is gone.

**Did the Fire Really Go Out?**

The flame is still there; it's just smoldering. When the therapists where Cynthia works hear a couple say, "The love is gone in our marriage," the therapist's view is, "No problem; that can be fixed." Quite simply there are road-blocks that have to be removed, and the therapists walk the couple past those obstacles, and sure enough, in most cases the flame that was once there is rekindled.

When Cynthia is teaching on sexual intimacy as part of a marriage seminar, she will often reference the concept "Sexual intimacy begins in the kitchen—when a man helps his wife with the chores of the home." Gentlemen, why adopt an "I've-already-conquered-her-there-is-no-need-for-more-romance" attitude, or become a self-centered, "give-me-what-I-need-when-I–need-it" individual while ignoring her emotional need for romance, affirmation, and communication? What's wrong with offering to help around the house? Why not be a hero to her from time to time?

### Dating Is Never Out of Style

Fanning the flames of romance includes setting aside time to be together. Dating, if you please. We have friends who build intentionality into their marriage by dating once a week. They live frenetic, gung-ho yet productive lives, but as a high priority, they set aside at least a couple of hours a week to get away from the hectic pace to go to a nearby restaurant for a cup of coffee, hot chocolate, or a piece of pie. Dating never goes out of style.

My wife, who was never an athlete, grew to love baseball. She was a Yankee fan since she was born and raised in or near New York City, then developed a love for Wrigley Field and the Chicago Cubs when we lived in a Chicago suburb for three years. Today she is a fan of our local double-A team, the Springfield Cardinals, a farm team of St. Louis. So guess where we often go to celebrate our anniversary? To a Cardinals game. It's a great date! She does the score sheet and everything. Baseball is a fun thing we do together because she made the effort to learn to enjoy it. That's the value of a date.

Learn a new skill set. For example, maybe a wife goes to a baseball game or fishing with her husband, and he goes shopping at the mall or to a theater production with her. That's the key to keeping the flame of romance burning. Do something intentional, do something to which you are not accustomed, do something fun, and do it together. It's the shared joy that is evidence of kindness. In fact, it is said to be the strongest evidence of all kindness characteristics.

### Surprise Your Spouse

Another way to keep the romance flame burning is unveiling a pleasant surprise from time to time. Surprise your spouse! Some make it a practice to do little nice things for their spouse, like putting a note in his laptop saying, "I love how you read a story to the kids at bedtime last night" or "Thank you for helping with the dishes after dinner last night. You are a caring person, and I love that about you!" Tell her, "I love how friendly you are with people." Place a couple of Hershey's chocolate kisses in her purse with a note and it will definitely create a warm fuzzy feeling in the brain and heart—and the stomach! Those "warm fuzzies" create an emotional link to your spouse that can help build a lasting marriage.

## A Quickie?

Don't limit your surprises to notes and chocolates, however. There are hundreds of ways to connect with your spouse that will make their day. How about a quickie? No, not that kind of quickie (though that's not a bad idea either). But you can always text or email a "quickie" note ("I noticed that you organized the papers on the kitchen table. That was nice of you—thank you") that will keep the flame burning. Cellphones can be a great tool for the three Cs—communication ("I'll be home in 20 minutes"), courtesy ("Do you need me to stop and pick up anything at the store?"), and connecting ("Hi, Sweetie, how is your day going?"). Communication quickies. They work.

Over time, these contacts build a bridge of understanding between spouses. It's not a control thing, it's a connection thing. That's what it's all about.

**Notes**
1. Rich Simon, "The Most Influential Therapists of the Past Quarter-Century," Psychotherapy Networker, March/April 2007.
2. Paula Vince, "The Vince Review," blog, March 22, 2017.
3. Emily Esfahani Smith, "Masters of Love," *The Atlantic Monthly* June 12, 2014.
4. Shaunti Feldhahn, *The Kindness Challenge: 30 Days to Improve Any Relationship* (Colorado Springs, CO: Waterbrook, 2016), 163.

# CHAPTER FIVE:

## Intimacy

## # 3. SEXUAL INTIMACY KEEPS US IN TUNE WITH EACH OTHER

### Ye Olde Wedding Vows

Becoming one flesh—what does it mean? Wedding vows have a long history dating back at least to the 1500s. Upon researching the various vows, I came across a fascinating footnote in Wikipedia regarding marriage ceremonies found in the Anglican Book of Common Prayer:

Upon agreement to marry, the Church of England usually offered couples a choice. The couple could promise each other to love and cherish or, alternatively, the groom promises to love, cherish, and worship and the bride to love, cherish, and obey.
The vows read: "With this Ring I thee wed, with my body I thee worship, and with all my worldly goods I thee endow: In the name of the Father, and of the Son, and of the Holy Ghost.

Amen."[1]

With my body I thee worship? What? When I first casually read it, I assumed that "with my body I worship you" was the woman's response in the vows. Then I noticed that on the contrary, it was the man's response, to "worship" his wife with his body! My wife was recently watching a 2016 BBC series (season 1, episode 5, "Victoria") about the marriage of the English Queen Victoria to Prince Albert in

1840, and the above rendition of the vows is used in the wedding scene. Fascinating!

There were many later revisions using other synonyms such as "adore" or "honor" instead of "worship." I can only assume that "worship" was too heavily laden a word to use since it generally applies to our relationship to God, but I find it quaint, yet perhaps more necessary today than ever, to make a lifelong commitment on the day of our wedding saying, "My bride, I love, cherish, and adore you and my body now belongs to you, and only to you, and with it I will honor and adore you as long as we both shall live."

Most marriage therapists would agree that sexuality, in all its dimensions, is a fundamental theme in counseling sessions, in part because it is intertwined with so many other aspects of our lives. When tough times come, tension and high negative emotions can affect our physical and sexual relationship. It is patently obvious that the sexual union between spouses is a powerful glue holding them together, and therefore it demands much care and special attention.

We will talk about *The Five Love Languages* later, but the core of the matter is that in physical and sexual intimacy, it is important to discover your spouse's love language and to learn to speak it. What turns her on? Or off? What arouses him? What shuts him down?

**Of Teapots and Microwaves**

For example, in the marriage seminars we conduct, Cynthia illustrates this fact in a PowerPoint with two items—a teapot on one side of the screen and a microwave on the other. The teapot represents most women, though not all: it takes time for the teapot to warm up and takes time to cool down. The microwave oven is like most males: it heats up rapidly and cooks quickly.

Of course this is a generality, and we must be careful not to put everyone in the same box. According to some statistics, in 20% of marriages it is the wife who has the greater sex drive. Yet in general terms we can talk about the male sex drive as being a greater force.

Teapots and microwaves aside, clinical studies demonstrate that generally men have a greater sex drive than women. In an article by Richard Sine in WebMD titled "Sex Drive: How Do Men and Women Compare?" Sine cites experts who say men score higher in libido, while women's sex drive is more fluid:

Birds do it, bees do it, and men do it any old time. But women will only do it if the candles are scented just right—and their partner has done the dishes first. A stereotype, sure, but is it true? Do men really have stronger sex drives than women?

Well, yes, they do. Study after study shows that men's sex drives are not only stronger than women's, but much more straightforward. The sources of women's libidos, by contrast, are much harder to pin down.

It's a common understanding that women place more value on emotional connection as a spark of sexual desire. But women also appear to be heavily influenced by social and cultural factors as well.

"Sexual desire in women is extremely sensitive to environment and context," says Edward O. Laumann, PhD. He is a professor of sociology at the University of Chicago and lead author of a major survey of sexual practices, *The Social Organization of Sexuality: Sexual Practices in the United States*.[2]

So in a sense, the teapot and microwave analogies are fairly on target, although again we must be careful not to overgeneralize.

I underscore this concept with a rather straightforward analogy from the wisest man who ever lived (besides Jesus). In Song of Solomon 7:6-8 (NIV), King Solomon says to his beloved wife—and notice how he appeals to her with words, even while acknowledging that he is attracted by what he sees: "How beautiful you are and how pleasing, my love, with your delights! Your stature is like that of the palm, and your breasts like clusters of fruit. I said, 'I will climb the palm tree; I will take hold of its fruit.'"

When I first noticed this particular verse, my thought was, That's a typical male response—I like what I see, I'll tell her how much I like it, then I will climb that tree and I will take hold of that fruit! At least he was wise enough to first romance her with flattering words.

Highly cited psychological researcher Roy Baumeister recently won a major lifetime achievement award from the Association for Psychological Science. Baumeister and two female colleagues in the late 1990s set to work reviewing hundreds of studies about human sexuality to attempt to determine whether the male sex drive was indeed stronger than that of females.

When he presented his hypothesis—that the male sex drive is stronger than the female drive—to peers in his field, they were skeptical. They believed, as Baumeister puts it, that "the idea that men have a stronger sex drive than women was probably some obsolete, wrong, and possibly offensive stereotype."[3] My guess is that they had absorbed a politically correct and trendy view of the matter. However, after researching hundreds of studies, Baumeister's team consistently found that women are less motivated by sex than men are. They found that for men, the goal of sex is sex itself.[4]

One 1996 study found that seven in ten men (70%), compared with four in ten women (40%), said the goal of sexual desire was simply having sex.[5] My observation is that when a man has an affair and says, "It meant nothing to me; it was just sex," he may in fact be telling the truth from his perspective, and that may be how he was treating his wife—no love and romance, it's just sex. In the same study, 35% of women said that love and intimacy were important goals of sex compared with 13% of men.[6]

Men also think about sex more, according to studies. When men and women monitor their sexual urges over a seven-day period, men report having twice as many sexual urges as women do. Men feel guiltier about sex. They feel guiltier... about thinking about sex more often than women do. For instance, men report having more unwanted and uncontrollable thoughts about sex. In one survey, men responded more affirmatively to the following statements than women did: "I think about sex more than I would like" and "I must fight to keep my sexual thoughts and behavior under control."[7]

The important factor is understanding who we are, how we are made, and how to manage our drives, feelings, emotions, and tendencies for the benefit of our spouse and ourselves and bring honor to the relationship. Face it—if we are sexually distancing ourselves from our spouse, male or female, it is tough to close the gap between us.

## Seeing or Hearing

Generally speaking, a woman is more inclined to respond to what she hears—it is an auditory response. Maybe it is because as a mother she is tuned in to the baby's cries more in the night, and as the primary nurturer, she has fine-tuned her response mechanism. Perhaps God hardwired her that way. Who knows?

She can also be aroused by what she hears from her partner. It's why sweet talk works so well. Kind, flattering, or seductive words can trigger a response in a woman.

A man tends to be more visual and aroused by what he sees. This underscores the importance of monitoring not just how we speak (kindly? harshly? disparagingly?) but also how we present ourselves (modestly? flirtingly? lustfully?) or what we watch or look at. One of the ancient writers in the Old Testament of the Holy Bible, Job, whose book is named after him, made it clear for us millennia ago: "I made a covenant with my eyes not to look lustfully at a young woman" (Job 31:1, NIV). Obviously lust and temptation are not new themes! Job committed to "averting," which the Cambridge Dictionary defines as

1. To prevent something bad from happening; avoid, as in, "He narrowly averted disaster."
2. To turn away your eyes or thoughts. This action is quite intentional and means "to look the other way."[8]

Turn away your eyes and avoid something bad; it's what Job vowed to do.

Just for clarity and fairness, a woman must avert as well—no gazing with lust at slim hips, a muscled body, or ripped abs. Men, no undressing a female with your eyes, gawking at cleavage or curves. And both genders should take care about how they present themselves in public. It's called modesty, an almost forgotten virtue in our society and culture today.

## "How Much Sex Does a Man Need?"

It was the written question a woman posed to Shaunti Feldhahn, the previously cited writer and speaker. Her answer was intriguing. She countered with her own question, "How many times do you need your husband to tell you 'I love you'?"[9] If he spouts the classic retort: 'Look, the day we were married, I told you I loved you. If anything changes, I'll let you know!' you might be headed for dangerous territory.

One might say that women are sexual beings but perhaps it takes longer for them to warm up. The concept of foreplay is not just physical for a woman, but emotional, verbal, and relational as well. If women are more prone to respond to what they hear, doesn't it make sense that when your words belittle, criticize, or demean her, or you are caustic and verbally abusive to her, she will have little interest in responding to you sexually? You aren't speaking her language, so she has a diminished interest in speaking yours!

I watched a *Celebrity Family Feud* episode with Shaquille O'Neill and Charles Barkley, two top-tier National Basketball Association players in their day competing on the show. Barkley was the first up, and Steve Harvey asked the first question: "We asked one hundred married women, If it were up to you, how many nights a week would you make love?" I was immediately intrigued and had my own idea of an answer. Barkley's answer was, "Three." Fair enough.

Shaq was next, same question. His answer was "Four." Now I was curious to know what one hundred married women would say! By the way, Barkley's answer got him 20 points, and Shaq's added 14 points.[10]

What was the number one answer? Once a week! That was a surprise. Both Shaq and Charles were shocked, you could see it on their faces, and I'm sure many men viewers were likewise surprised. It does illustrate the different points of view that exist on the subject of human sexuality, and above all it shows how important it is to know your spouse and to know yourself when it comes to sexual intimacy.

Is once in a lifetime enough to be told, "I love you"? If one hundred married women were surveyed, what would they say? Or one hundred men? Is once a year enough, or a once a month, or once a week? How much is enough if verbal assurance of love is your love language? Maybe sex isn't her definition of affirming physical touch, or saying

"Thank you" doesn't slip off her tongue easily. Maybe he isn't accustomed to saying "I love you" like she wishes he would, but if you both know how important it is to the other person, it would bring pleasure both to you and to your spouse as you learn to do what pleases the other.

So, men, it's time to start investing in your relationship. Stop seeing things just from your point of view and start exploring how she sees things. Ladies, the same rule applies—figure out what is meaningful to him and put it into practice.

As Feldhahn states, "One of a man's deepest emotional needs is to feel that his wife desires him."[11] A woman's greatest need is to know she is loved and wanted. In Song of Solomon 7:10 (NIV), Solomon's loved one so succinctly puts it, "I belong to my beloved, and his desire is for me."

For a man oftentimes "A roll in the hay means all is okay." Likewise one could say for the wife, "When 'I love you' is spoken, our bond is unbroken." Forgive my feeble attempt at poetry, but you get the idea.

According to numerous researchers, about 100 million couples around the world have sex every day. So whether you are a teapot or a microwave, we trust you have learned, or have determined to learn, what will bring the most joy to your spouse.

## Is Sex Evil?

A note to those who believe that God frowns upon sex, that it is something inherently evil—it is not! God designed the sexual components in the male and female anatomy even before sin entered the world. He saw that it was good. Love stories abound in the Scriptures, like the love story of Isaac and Rebekah in Genesis, the heartwarming account of Ruth and Boaz in the book of Ruth, and the highly romantic previously mentioned book of Song of Solomon with the spicy interchanges with the king and his beloved. One can't read these stories and not be moved by the pure romance therein.

It goes without saying that sexual intimacy is a delicate subject. It is surprising and sometimes even alarming how marriages can lapse into what is known as a low-sex or no-sex relationship. I've asked therapists about this, and I'm told that Dr. Clifford Penner and Joyce Penner, respected sex therapists, addressed this kind of marriage in a workshop. The Penners say they do not initially ask, "How many times do you have sex?" They do ask about how the couple kisses (do they kiss, how often, are they enjoying it?). Eventually the issue of sex or lack thereof surfaces on its own.

## # 4. PHYSICAL TOUCH HELPS BONDING

Obviously, physical touch is vital to the romantic and sexual experience. It is also important to everyday interactions. Let's unwrap this.

### Oxytocin, the "Bonding Hormone"

Oxytocin is a neurotransmitter, or neuropeptide, in the brain and is known as the "bonding" element (not technically a hormone). It is released through physical touch and causes both physiological and behavioral effects when released in the body. Oxytocin is produced in the hypothalamus of the brain and is released into the bloodstream via the pituitary gland. It evokes feelings of contentment, trust, empathy, calmness, and security and reduces anxiety and fear. Under certain circumstances, oxytocin can hinder the release of cortisol, or stress hormones.[12]

It helps the brain process information and feelings and can create warmth and trust. Several surveys have been conducted to understand the role of this neurotransmitter in life, especially in terms of faith, trust, and morality, where it seems to play a role. We await those findings. What we do know is that oxytocin is released in the body when a person considers himself or herself to be secure, safe, and connected to their loved ones. Through the release of this chemical, the brain knows that everything is safe and that there is no need to worry—thus the bonding.

In a book by Bryan A. Sands, *Everyone Love Sex: So Why Wait?: A Discussion in Sexual Faithfulness*, the author humorously describes this neurotransmitter: "Oxytocin promotes bonding and attachment, and if all the hormones had an opportunity to vote for the 'most popular' award in the hormone yearbook, its peers would vote for it every time because it makes others feel good and close when it is active."[13]

Oxytocin has been dubbed the "cuddle hormone" (though technically a neurotransmitter) because it creates bonding, trust, and generosity in us. In fact, whenever you feel comfort or security, oxytocin is involved. It affects every form of human bonding.

## What Triggers the Release of Oxytocin in the Brain?

So what causes the release of oxytocin in the brain? This is where it gets interesting. Here are at least eight triggers that release oxytocin:

1. Hugging
2. Snuggling, cuddling (thus the importance of a mom or dad carrying the child in a pouch or holder on their chest, face to face, and not like a papoose on the back). Cuddling gets those neurotransmitters flowing in your brain.
3. Arousal and orgasms
4. Labor in childbirth
5. Breastfeeding (oxytocin is produced in pregnancy, levels increase significantly during

active labor and childbirth, and both mom and baby produce oxytocin after birth and as long as baby breastfeeds)
6. Massages—a massage between husband and wife can be a great turn-on and healthy for developing closeness.
7. Dancing—again, closeness is the key here. Beware of dancing with those of the opposite gender. Keep it "at home."
8. Praying to God. Believe it or not, praying activates the same brain function and release of oxytocin as does sexual activity, which is a strong argument for couples praying together and at the same time a caution to exercise care when one prays for someone else of the opposite sex.

It is obvious by reviewing this list that these activities would have a sense of closeness attached to them. All trigger a release of warmth and a feeling of well-being in us and in others, an inherently positive activity if one is careful to keep it within the bounds of those for whom this contact is warranted (babies, children, spouse, loved ones).

**The Twenty-Second Hug**

Lindsay Kellner, senior wellness and beauty editor at mindbodygreen.com, on January 5, 2017, observed the following about a popular and growing social phenomenon, the twenty-second hug:

I first heard about the 20-second hug through Sadie Lincoln, founder and CEO of barre3. With two kids, a husband of 16 years, and a booming business to run, Sadie is one of the busiest ladies in wellness. As someone who runs her company alongside her husband, they're always "checking boxes together," as she explained. It's super easy for any conversation to turn into a work one, which can put out even the fieriest of flames in a hot second.

One way they've been able to keep themselves individually sane and simultaneously reconnect every day is by doing the 20-second hug. Every morning before work, they hug for a full 20 seconds. "I can't even believe its effects, and now we both crave it. It's so nourishing. I can feel his heartbeat; we both calm down when we slow down and realize what matters. We are here to witness life together."

Another reason she loves it? They do it out in the open on purpose, so the kids see it, setting an excellent example of how loving home life can be.

Hugging is one of the oldest and finest methods of connecting to others and building trust. Scientists and researchers have confirmed that yes, a hug does indeed trigger a release of oxytocin and, yes, oxytocin is responsible for trust and positive relationships. Everyone has at least 20 seconds.[14]

When doing marriage seminars, Cynthia and I challenge the couples to do the twenty-second hug. Often she and I will illustrate it and occasionally, especially if it is a couples retreat, we all stand and hug our spouse. It is fun and productive, and, as Kellner said, we can all spare twenty seconds!
We will talk later about non-sexual physical touch and what it means to "touchers" when we talk about the five love languages. Do you have a friend or loved one who is a "toucher" and can't communicate without using their hands? We do too. For them touch is essential. It's a toucher's way to process the universe around them. But touch is not only for touchers—all of us, one way or another, thrive on touches. It is a proven fact that a newborn baby that is never held or caressed

will lack certain hormones that help them grow. We never outgrow our need for tactile interaction.

## # 5. PLACE YOUR SPOUSE HIGHER ON THE LADDER OF LIFE

The Bible says that with "humility of mind regards one another as more important than yourselves" (Philippians 2:3, NASB). Not equal to me—more important, better! Everyone has something of value that I don't have but which I should at least acknowledge. Let's face it, it's hard to be humble and submissive when I have problems seeing the value or the good in the other person.

**Humility: Hard to Learn but Highly Rewarding**

Grappling with this and learning the lesson of humility was perhaps one of the seminal moments in my life and career. Had I not learned it—and it is still a daily challenge—I would never have survived in the years that followed, much less thrived in the various aspects of my life. In fact I believe I would have failed miserably.

I spent one year on staff at a church. The prospects looked good when we arrived. My lead pastor and we seemed to get along well. Soon, however, we began to take exception to observations and commentaries from him that made us bristle. Although he was the authority in our lives, we were feeling controlled and unappreciated. A crisis loomed.

At the point of impending relational disaster, I ran across a booklet by a well-known charismatic speaker named Bob Mumford titled, "The Problem of Doing Your Own Thing."[15] Mumford wrote it in the early 1970s. It is a small book and is still available online. In a nutshell it was a teaching on the problem we have with that thing residing in all of us from the time we were born—the problem of independence, of "turning each one to our own way" and always looking out for number one. Mumford's solution was straightforward—accept and submit to the authorities God has placed over you. That is almost impossible to do without a change in how we view that authority figure. Admittedly, Mumford later got off on a "Shepherding" tangent as an extreme application of this principle (which he later acknowledged), but the essence of it still holds.

Mumford quotes Jesus' words when he wept over Jerusalem saying, "Jerusalem, Jerusalem, you who kill the prophets and stone those sent to you, how often have I longed to gather your children together, as a hen gathers her checks under her wings, and you were not willing. For I tell you, you will not see me again until you say, 'Blessed is he who comes in the name of the Lord'" (Matthew 23:36-39, NIV).

In other words, God has sent this person in his name—his son Jesus in this case—and they rejected him and so their "house" was to remain empty and desolate until they could embrace him as the one sent to them as God's representative.

That was God speaking to me. I was the one who had the problem, not my pastor. In effect I had reserved for myself the right to decide when, how, and to whom I would submit, and therein lay the problem. God had never made me the judge, nor was he inclined to do so. I was not allowed to make the call, so until I could humble myself, call "blessed" the authority figure over me, and do whatever I was asked to do, embracing the person and the task I was given, I would remain empty of God's presence. I decided then and there to say, "Whatever my pastor says to do, I will do it. If he says 'shine my shoes,' I embrace it and do it willingly." It began the transforming process in my life.

More than forty-five years later, that lesson has served me well in many facets of my life and ministry. Humility does not come easily, and I still have not arrived, but when I accept and welcome that person, saying, "Blessed is he (or she) who comes to me as God's representative," then everything falls into place. Interestingly, I had four main portfolios in that church, and from that critical moment on, every one of them grew impressively. It was God who made it happen but only when I was able to embrace His way and His leadership in my life.

So it's not difficult to deduce from this that if we should esteem all others better, then we most certainly should esteem our spouse better than ourselves. Perhaps Abbot Christopher Jamison, in *Finding Happiness: Monastic Steps for a Fulfilling Life*, defines the subject best when he compares pride as "self-importance" and humility as "an honest approach to the reality of our own lives and acknowledges that we are *not* more important than other people."[16] Well said.

## The Specialness Plague

Sadly, our selfie-plagued world today abounds with people whose sense of self-importance knows no limits, like the famous actor who demanded a raise to three million dollars per episode of his hit sitcom on television declaring, "I'm tired of pretending I'm not special!"

But esteeming our wives better? That's not as easy as one would think, is it, gentlemen? In our male-driven, man-entitled macho world we don't easily think that way. "Husbands, love your wives." That's fairly straightforward, isn't it? Love her like Christ loves the church. In fact, love her like you love yourself. Make her the special one. Serve her for a change. Doesn't the Bible say, "In this same way, husbands ought to love their wives as their own bodies. He who loves his wife loves himself. After all, no one ever hated their own body, but they feed and care for their body, just as Christ does the church" (Ephesians 5:28-29, NIV).

To be sure, most men are quick to quote verses about how a woman should submit to the man but conveniently overlook the way a man should love, care for, and esteem his wife.

Likewise the wife should take seriously how she should honor and respect her husband and esteem him for the qualities he has that are better than hers in some way. It's easy to disparage and belittle but much harder to esteem and affirm the good in the other person. How do we esteem our spouse better than ourselves?

**So Where Do I Start?**

Start by asking God for help in seeing your spouse in a different way.

As necessary, realign your thinking regarding how you view your spouse. In our marriage enrichment seminars we sometimes ask couples to write a list of those qualities about their spouse that are unique or positive. It's a great way to begin.

It is interesting in these settings how often a couple will struggle to find words to describe the spouse. Inevitably he may say something like, "She's a good cook," or "She's a hard worker around the house," or "She plays the piano very well." Or she will say, "He makes a good living," or "He makes sure that the car runs well and is always gassed up," or "He fixes things around the house when they break down."

That's when we will push them a little by saying, "That's good, but describe something about them as a person—who he or she *is* more than what he or she *does*." That's when they struggle. We are all conditioned to evaluate appearance and performance more than character, and activities more than virtues. Character goes to the core of who one is as a person.

Let's face it, even though at the beginning of your relationship you might have thought "She's so hot!" or "She's the life of the party," or perhaps "He's such a stud!"

or "What a charmer!" the fact is, it may not last. Looks can be fleeting, but character will always win the prize.

Make it a point not only to rearrange your thinking but also to put your "esteem of the other person" into practice in some way.

Verbalizing virtues is always a positive step. For example, it's one thing to say, "That's a pretty dress" or "Good meal, thanks," but it's even more meaningful when a spouse says, "I noticed how attentive you are to the kids when they seem to need your attention; you're a really good father" or "I'm very proud of the way you were so kind when that clerk in the store snapped at you; it shows that you are a good and patient person."

In these illustrations, goodness, kindness, and patience are projected as qualities the other person has demonstrated, and they are the product of the Holy Spirit's working in their lives so they are qualitatively better than what they wear or how they cook. The character traits and virtues are important as positive markers in a person's life. Learn to highlight and value them.

When you notice and comment on who your spouse is as a human being, it impacts their self-esteem and makes them want to live up to the really good person you see in them and that they want to see in themselves. It works with our kids, and it works with our spouse. The more often you can find ways to finish these sentences, such as "I just love the way that you _____," or "I'm proud of you when you_____," the more often you will think more highly of the other person and build their self-esteem in the process.

Then do it. Find a way to help tangibly, lift up, or prioritize the preferences of your spouse. It's tiring to hear, "Oh, I hate shopping, I'll never go to the mall with my wife!" Why not? It can be more than fun; it can be a learning experience as well.

Cynthia values my opinion on what she buys to wear. After all, I'm the one who is looking at her. We shop together, compare notes, and look for bargains. She knows she can buy whatever she wants whenever she wants to (up to our predetermined mutual limit), but by the same token, she is careful with the finances and never overspends. I like going to a department store and walking through the aisles while she's trying on something in the fitting room, and sometimes I'll see a woman in the store looking at me quizzically, like "Mister, are you in the wrong department?" But I try to find something to bring to Cynthia that I think she will like to try on. Every now and then, bingo, we both agree. Shopping together strengthens our bond, and I learn about Cynthia's taste in clothes. It's a good deal!

## Mother Teresa

Shane Claiborne in his book *Irresistible Revolution* states that often people ask him what Mother Teresa was like since he writes about her:

> Sometimes it is like they wonder if she glowed in the dark or had a halo. She was short, wrinkled, and precious, maybe even a little ornery, like a beautiful, wise old granny.

> But there is one thing I will never forget—her feet. Her feet were deformed. Each morning I would stare at them. I wondered if she had contracted leprosy.

> One day a Sister explained, "Her feet are deformed because we get just enough donated shoes for everyone, and Mother does not want anyone to get stuck with the worst pair, so she digs through and finds them. And years of doing that

have deformed her feet." Years of loving her neighbor as herself deformed her feet.

When people are asked about the person whose life they most admire, so often the answer is "Mother Teresa." She made the most of her life. It is a paradox, because her life was a life of self-denial, taking up her cross and following Jesus.[17]

Mother Teresa found a practical way to esteem others better than herself. She intentionally chose the poorest shoes so that no one else need wear them. Her feet were deformed but her inner person stood tall. Your feet may feel it, but your inner person will grow stronger and taller too.

**Listening to Your Wife Opens Doors of Understanding**

Gentlemen, pay attention to your wife. Listen to her. Dr. John Gottman was interviewed on CNN a few years back and made this statement: "If you want success in your life, listen to your wife!" Sounds like a setup for a joke, but it isn't.

When God decided to help Adam, who had been very self-reliant up to that point, he made a woman, Eve, as a helpmeet. God knew Adam needed help. "Meet" means "fitting, ideal," and of course "help" means "helper." She was his ideal helper. In the original Hebrew language, the word *helper* was Ezer, which was a name for God and from which is derived Eben-ezer, "hitherto has the Lord helped us." God is our Ezer, our helper, and so is the woman he gave us.

Don't you think God knew what he was doing? Or did he know how different the man and the woman were and knew what each one needed? She needed to respect him, he needed to take heed and pay attention to her and to recognize that she was often the nearest—though not the only—voice of God to him.

Women often are more sensitive, active listeners, in tune with emotions and feelings. Were they made that way? To a great extent, yes. Generally, men are more action-oriented, doers, builders, gatherer-hunters, fixers—in short, more inclined toward behavior and action. Not always, but generally so.

But think about it. It makes sense. If you have a child, a woman carried that child in her womb for nine months. Every day she was in tune with her growing tummy, aware of another human being forming within her. All her senses are fine tuned to the well-being of that child. After the baby is born, she is acutely aware of the baby's needs, feeding it, changing diapers, kissing it, holding it in her arms and generally giving affection.

Generally, men tend toward allowing the wife and mother of their child to be the nurturer, and it makes a lot of sense. However, the wife/mother should not be the only nurturer or caregiver. That newborn needs both the female and the male input into their lives to become a healthy and well-balanced human being. That baby needs not only to know that the sweet, kind, soft-spoken, soft-faced big person holding them is there for them, but that the other big, deep-voiced, scratchy-faced person also loves them.

I am not off track if I intentionally pay attention to my wife. She is intuitive and sensitive, yet strong and self-reliant. My decision and will to listen to her opens the door for God to direct me with insight and perspectives I might not have on my own. As one counselor put it, listening is not just with our ears, but with our hearts. We all benefit from that arrangement.

"But I'm supposed to be the priest in the home," he might say. What did the priests in the Bible do? They facilitated, they helped others get closer to God. You can help her get closer to God, and she will help you. We learn in the New Testament that God has made us all "kings and priests unto God" (Revelation 1:6, KJV). God has made us that way in Christ.

## Notes
1. "The Book of Common Prayer," en.wikipedia.org/wiki/Marriage vows; John Baskerville is credited as the original author of the vows.
2. Richard Sine, "Sex Drive: How Do Men and Women Compare?" WebMD, www.webmd.com/.../sex-drive-how-do-men-women-compare.
3. Emily Esfahani Smith, "How Strong Is the Female Sex Drive After All?" *The Atlantic*, July 2, 2013, https://www.theatlantic.com/sexes/archive/2013/07/how-strong-is-the-female-sex-drive-after-all/277429/.
4. Esfahani Smith.
5. Esfahani Smith.
6. Esfahani Smith.
7. Esfahani Smith.
8. The Cambridge Dictionary, Cambridge University Press, dictionary.cambridge.org/dictionary/english/avert.
9. Shaunti Feldhahn, "How Often Do Men Need to Have Sex?" Shaunti Feldhahn, May 4, 2015, https://shaunti.com/2015/05/how-often-do-men-need-to-have-sex/.
10. *Celebrity Family Feud*, ABC network, aired June 17, 2018.
11. Feldhahn.
12. "Oxytocin in Childbirth: A Labor of Love," Health Foundations Birth Center, November 1, 2013, https://www.health-foundations.com/blog/2013/11/01/oxytocin-in-childbirth-a-labor-of-love.
13. Bryan A. Sands, *Everyone Loves Sex: So Why Wait: A Discussion in Sexual Faithfulness* (Abilene, TX: Leafwood Publishers, 2017).
14. Lindsay Kellner, senior wellness and beauty editor at mindbodygreen.com, January 5, 2017, mindbodygreen.com.
15. Bob Mumford, *The Problem of Doing Your Own Thing* (Wilmington, DE: Christian Growth Ministries, 1972).
16. Abbot Christopher Jamison, *Finding Happiness: Monastic Steps for a Fulfilling Life* (Worth Abbey, Sussex, England: Liturgical Press, 2009).
17. Shane Claiborne, *Irresistible Revolution* (Grand Rapids, MI: Zondervan, 2016).

# CHAPTER SIX:

## Conquering the Giants

### # 6. OVERCOME ANGER, ABUSE, AND ADULTERY

The truth is that esteeming our spouse and affirming their positive qualities is a skill we can and should develop. But there is another side to the concept, and this would be a good place to talk about how we handle the betrayals or failures of our spouse. These are tough subjects, but they must be addressed. I'm talking about three huge issues that couples deal with that should be added to the "male privilege" or "entitlement" baggage that seems to plague many of us.

However, though men may face these personal giants, they are by no means exclusive traits of the male species, as we will see.

These next three battleground issues deal with a temperament trait, a behavioral pattern, and a character flaw—and they seem to surface in many settings where marital conflict is involved. They are anger, abuse, and adultery.

**A Temperament Trait: Anger**
*Why Are Angry People Angry?*

Not long ago our family reunion with the kids and grandkids included a day at a large amusement park near where we live. As I was waiting for them to finish an hour-long excursion through a cave, I tried to relax a little in a shop where they sell everything unique to the park. The entrance and exit to the cave started inside the shop.

As I waited, I heard a high-pitched, very shrill scream coming from the other end of the store. I thought, "Here we go!" The minutes passed, and I knew this young child would surely wear out. He didn't. I commented to the lady standing nearby that the child must not be very happy. I was so glad I didn't say what I was really thinking—because she was his grandmother. Soon I saw the mother and another family member walk him by in his stroller. He was still screaming. I wanted to see if there was any attempt to calm him. There wasn't. I can safely say that here was an example of an angry man in the making. No discipline, no words, no calming influence—just let him be angry. I wonder what he will be like in twenty years.

I remember once stomping my foot in anger and my mother giving me *that look* that said, "Don't you *ever* do that again!" That certainly got my attention, and with gentle reminders from others from time to time throughout my life, I have become a better person for it.

Frankly I'm not certain why there are so many angry men in the world. It's not that all the guys go around yelling, punching the walls, or throwing cooking pans across the room, but there is something peculiar about a man's psyche that sometimes erupts in anger that lashes out and physically, verbally, or emotionally wants to damage the other person. Or it simmers in a slow boil until, sometime, somewhere . . . boom!

In Louie Giglio's book, *Goliath Must Fall*, the author makes his point like this:

> Ask someone if he or she is an angry person and most will deny it at first. "I don't go around in a rage every day," they'll say. "I don't yell at people I work with. I don't lash out at my wife or throw things around the house."
>
> But dig under the top layer of our lives just a bit and it can be a different story. Sometimes the anger

emerges overtly. Sometimes the anger is there, but it isn't seen for a long, long time. The anger lurks underneath the surface, waiting for the right spark to set it off…Most anger is rooted in some form of rejection. Something was or wasn't said. Something was repeatedly done to us. Something we deserved but were deprived of. A hurt. A wound. A stab. What do we do about this giant of anger?[1]

Perhaps the greatest irony of this phenomenon of angry men is captured in the title of Paul Hegstrom's *Angry Men and the Women Who Love Them: Breaking the Cycle of Physical and Emotional* Abuse.[2]

It would seem to be obvious to an outsider that there is a deep-seated problem in a marriage scarred by anger. But the reality is that for a variety of reasons, often there is also a powerful emotional dependency between an angry or abusive husband and his wife. Without question it is a complex relationship, but there can be a resolution to the anger problem.

What is the root of the problem? How does a boy develop into an angry man? PsychGuides.com posts some insightful views on anger symptoms and causes and effects that might help us.

## Anger Disorders

According to a study conducted by the Harvard Medical School, nearly 8% of adolescents display anger issues that qualify for lifetime diagnoses of intermittent explosive disorder.[3] Anger issues aren't limited to teens, and it is important to understand anger symptoms and causes and effects if you suspect you are, or someone you know is, suffering from an anger disorder.

Individuals who have trouble controlling anger or who experience anger outside of a normal emotional range can manifest different types of anger disorders. Different experts have published contradicting lists of anger types, but some widely accepted forms of anger include

- Chronic anger, which is prolonged, can impact the immune system and be the cause of other mental disorders [the kid screaming?];
- Passive anger, which doesn't always come across as anger and can be difficult to identify [simmering];
- Overwhelmed anger, which is caused by life demands that are too much for an individual to cope with;
- Self-inflicted anger, which is directed toward the self and may be caused by feelings of guilt [perhaps more prevalent than we know];
- Judgmental anger, which is directed toward others and may come with feelings of resentment;
- Volatile anger, which involves sometimes spontaneous bouts of excessive or violent anger.[4]

These fall into the disorder category. But not all anger is a disorder. What about relationships plagued by irritability, frustration, or loud outbursts? Gary Chapman, the author of *The Five Love Languages*, addressed this in a recent Internet blurb:

> Why do people get angry? I believe we get angry when our sense of "right" is violated. When this happens, it can lead us to one of two types of anger:
>
> - Definitive anger: when someone has wronged us
> - Distorted anger: when things didn't go our way

Much of the anger people experience is distorted anger. The traffic moved slowly. Our spouse didn't do things the way we wanted. This kind of anger, however, can still be very intense and must be processed. Ask yourself, "Would it be helpful if I shared my anger with someone? In sharing it, might I improve things for everyone? If not, should I simply let it go?"[5]

Whatever you do, do something positive. Don't hold your anger inside. Anger was meant to be a visitor, not a resident. Processing your anger in a positive way will lead you toward freedom, emotional health, and relational stability.

*A Visitor or a Resident?*

Chapman said it well: anger was meant to be a visitor, not a resident. The Bible likewise says not to let the sun go down on your anger (wrath). Resolve the anger issue; don't let it fester.

Any therapist will tell you that anger is not a primary emotion but a secondary one. That's very important to understand. Reading these lists of the different kinds of anger, we can see the feelings beneath the surface that trigger an angry reaction. Underneath every eruption of anger there is a "button," normally a fear button that has been pushed that drives us to frustration, irritability, high anxiety, extreme disappointment in ourselves, fear of failure or abandonment, confusion, or a host of other negatives that lie buried inside us since our childhood. When someone, especially our spouse, pushes that button, unintentionally or otherwise, the common reaction is anger.

When anger manifests itself it is normal to blame the other person—"You made me angry and I couldn't help it!" However, the "anger trigger" is inside of you in the form of a deep-seated fear, and often those layers need to be peeled back, like the layers of an onion, so that understanding and healing can bring restoration to our relationships.

This is why at the Focus Marriage Institute in Branson, Missouri, the therapists help each couple chart their own unique fear cycle to guide them in better understanding why they react the way they do. I believe it is one of the most revealing and profitable components of the counseling intensives that are offered there and crucial to the success of couples wanting to restore hope to their marriage.

Though I do not have all the answers, I do know that unless we learn how to manage the anger issue in ourselves, it will drive us apart from our spouse instead of draw us closer to each other.

Let me encourage you—there is hope. There is a peace that God gives that serves as a referee in our hearts ("Let the peace of God rule in your hearts," Colossians 3:15, NIV). That word *rule* literally means to "be the arbiter or referee." If God's peace rules in your heart, anger will disappear.

*Arthur's Story*

My wife grew up on Long Island, New York, one of two daughters of Scandinavian immigrant parents. Her mother was Norwegian, her father a Swede, both from the old country. Her dad came out of a rough background, a tough guy, a boxer, and a man given to explosive anger. And he was an alcoholic. With just months to live according to doctors (due to heavy drinking), he found his way into a Norwegian Pentecostal church in Brooklyn where he was saved, healed, and filled with the Holy Spirit.

From then on Arthur Holmberg shared his testimony of deliverance from sin and alcohol to hundreds of people who needed hope and change in their lives. The church was filled with people who, because of Arthur, had new life and new hope.

The irony was that Arthur, though a believer with a dramatic salvation testimony, was still an angry man. My wife, her sister, and their mother all knew the reality of the fury of that one area of Arthur's life that was never yielded to God, one he kept for himself. I said there is hope, and there is. Arthur's life proves it. When Arthur was eighty years old and beset by a variety of physical ills that eventually ended his life at eighty-three, God did one of the most miraculous works of grace ever—he helped Arthur conquer and release that anger monster in him. Thea, his wife and my mother-in-law, shared with Cynthia the whole work of grace that God did in Cynthia's dad. He died an emotionally whole person, at peace with himself, his wife, his family, and his heavenly Father.

My friend, there is hope for you. It matters not how long you've fought your battle. God is waiting for you to surrender that meanness, anger, and toxic nastiness to him. He will make you the person you really want to be, down deep inside. Why not yield sooner rather than later? You will never regret it.

There are resources on anger management that provide good tools. They will help you learn to take control of your anger and manage it properly. Look them up.

## A Behavioral Pattern: Abuse

*The Macho Man*

A few years back during the course of planning for some of our marriage seminars in Latin America, I looked up the word *machismo*. It is an intriguing subject since the concept of male superiority, privilege, or entitlement is at the root of so many societal flaws. Truthfully, I was shocked at how direct and strongly worded was the definition I found in the *Dictionary of Mexican Cultural Code Words* (it was in

Spanish, by the way). Take a look at machismo from the Mexican perspective; machismo is:

1. The repudiation of all "feminine" virtues such as unselfishness, kindness, frankness, and truthfulness.

2. Being willing to lie without compunction, to be suspicious, envious, jealous, malicious, vindictive, and brutal, and finally, to be willing to fight and kill without hesitation to protect one's manly image.

3. That a man could not let anything detract from his image of himself as a man's man, regardless of the suffering it brings on himself and the women around him.

4. The proof of every man's manliness is his ability to completely dominate his wife and children, to have sexual relations with any woman he wants.

5. Never let anyone question, diminish, or attempt to thwart his manhood.

6. Never reveal his true feelings to anyone lest they somehow take advantage of him.[6]

The bluntness of this definition got my attention, especially since it came from a Latin country where they are normally very suave in their expressions, a trait I admire. But it underscores an aspect of manhood that expresses itself in fistfights, cursing, throwing objects, and the abusive behavior we see in so many movies and television programs today. This sets the table for the subject of domestic abuse, since abuse and machismo are first cousins, so to speak.

Abuse is not an exclusive trait to any culture, nor is machismo or anger. It is imbedded in human nature. Though not exclusive to men, abuse is more normally associated with the male of the species. At least 85% of domestic abuse cases are perpetrated by men.[7]

There may be various contributing factors to the prevalence of machismo and male domination. However, when one reviews human history, it is hard to escape the single factor of war and conquest, domination, and the subsequent license to rule and control that resulted from these conquests. Whether they were Philistines, Babylonians, Egyptians, Assyrians, Greeks, Romans, Mongols, Vikings, Spaniards, or the English, each conquering empire imposed itself on the vanquished armies, often with unleashed impulses to enslave, pillage, plunder, rape, and abuse at will.

In José L. González's book *Machismo y Matriarcado: Raíces Tóxicas de Nuestra Cultura y Su Antídoto: Ser Transformados por el Pacto* (*Machismo and Matriarchy: The Toxic Roots of Our Culture and Its Antidote: Being Transformed by the Covenant*), the author makes his case that the major impact on the Spanish culture comes from the conquest of the new world. After all, the Spanish were called *conquistadores* (conquerors) for a reason. Writes Alberto Montessi in the prologue: "I agree with González in affirming that [the conquistadores] were profoundly attracted by the indigenous sexuality. The European psyche literally exploded at the possibility of free and unbridled sexual activity. The woman was part of the plunder."[8]

It is not difficult to see how that theme has played out in empire after empire as conquering hordes prevailed on each continent. In the Americas they came to conquer, control, colonize, convert, and civilize. Even conversion to Christianity or the civilizing of the natives was sometimes abusive, though not always.

What is the nature of abuse? There are various types of abuse, such as the obvious physical abuse, emotional and psychological abuse, or sexual abuse. In many cases society has condoned such abuse, or at least not condemned such action, and worse yet, even blamed the victim.

Abuse can be situational (one case), systematic (a regular occurrence), or systemic (perhaps a general practice of a society, culture, or family group). It often begins at a young age, both for the victim as well as for the future perpetrator. It is not uncommon for kids to make fun of, ridicule, or taunt their peers. To this day I can clearly remember a colleague in high school calling me names I cannot repeat here, hurtful names. It seems that this kind of verbal jabbing has escalated significantly in today's culture and has emerged as one of the alarming traits plaguing our schools.

*Bullying*

This tendency to harass is referred to as bullying, either physical or now cyber-bullying, where students verbally abuse or haze another student, sometimes with tragic consequences.

DoSomething.org is a global movement of six million young people intent on making positive change, online and off, regarding bullying in schools. Here are a few facts they publish:

- Over 3.2 million students are victims of bullying each year.
- Approximately 160,000 teens skip school every day because of bullying.
- 17% of American students report being bullied 2 to 3 times a month or more within a school semester.
- 1 in 4 teachers see nothing wrong with bullying and will intervene only 4% of the time.[9]

Dare I say it? Unless profound societal changes kick in, we can foresee a whole generation of angry people infecting society at large and creating an abusive culture.

Since over 85% of abuse cases involve men as perpetrators, I will use the masculine gender as the abusive person but with the understanding that not all abusers are men.

The definition of abuse is uncomplicated: abuse occurs when the man begins to exercise power over the woman in such a manner as it causes harm or injury to her, increases her responsibilities, and creates a situation of privilege for him.

Domestic abuse grows out of attitudes and values, not feelings. This is extremely important. It is easy to blame negative feelings, when in fact the culprit is wrong thinking and beliefs. The bully in school believes certain behavior is permissible and that he or she can therefore act with impunity.

*The Tree of Abuse*

One useful illustration of these attitudes and values is that of a tree, the Tree of Abuse, provided for us by a friend and colleague, a woman who suffered abuse which ultimately led to a divorce:

- The roots of the tree are based in the concept that she is my property (she is mine, my woman, and I own her);
- The trunk of the tree is the idea that I have the right to do what I do to her (like the child who runs at his mother and hits her repeatedly with his fists—until he is shown that he does not have that right);
- The branches of the tree are the idea that I must control her, that she needs me to do this to her.

These are beliefs and attitudes that ultimately express themselves in abuse. We all have our own set of ideas, concepts, values, beliefs, and attitudes. They determine our behavior, and the composite of all of these determine the kind of people that we are. A rude person believes that he or she has the right to be rude; a verbal abuser believes that he or she has that prerogative; likewise a cheater believes he or she is thus entitled. All abusive behavior stems from wrong thinking and attitudes.

How many times have you heard of accounts of people who seemed to be nice enough on the job, downtown, in church, or at the store, but when the reality of that person's abusive behavior at home eventually surfaces, others are surprised. "But he seemed to be such a nice guy!" Don't be fooled.

The Branches:
  She needs me to control her

The Trunk:
  I have a right to do this

The Roots:
  She's my property; I own her

*Figure 6.1: The Tree of Abuse*

We were doing a seminar in a South American country when I heard this account from a pastor, to whom another pastor confessed, "When I was about to marry my wife, my father [an abuser], on my wedding day, told me, 'Just beat her good the first night and after that, you won't have any more problems!'"

It's hard to believe: she's mine, I have a right to do this, and she needs me to control her. This is wrong thinking!

Abuse and respect are opposites. Abusers cannot change unless they overcome the total lack of respect toward their partner. Abusers are much more conscious of what they are doing than they appear to be, but in every case, their actions are prompted by their basic belief system and attitudes.

Often abusers are not disposed to quit being abusive. It is not that they are unable to stop abusing; they don't want to give up the power and the control over the other person. It's a choice they make. The woman doesn't cause the abuse, and she cannot stop it by discovering why he is abusive or what she can do to prevent it or how she can satisfy his emotional "needs." And it's time to put an end to the cultural tendency to blame the woman for "provoking" the abuse or feeling sorry for men who suffer the consequences of their abusive behavior. It's time to grow up societally!

Gentlemen, let's be gentle men. Let's be kind, tenderhearted, and forgiving. That is true manliness. That is what Jesus was—a real man, a gentle man. He invites us to "learn of me, for I am meek and lowly in heart" (Matthew 11:29, KJV). Gentleness is in short supply these days; let's lead the way by being gentle.

## A Character Flaw: Adultery

Nothing is more devastating than discovering that your spouse has had an affair, either ongoing or a one-time fling. Intriguingly, when we talk about cheating spouses, we often assume that it is the husband who is cheating, but neither spouse is exempt from the temptation to cheat.

*Sexual Addiction*

Counselors will tell us how frequently affairs and sexual addiction (SA) destabilize the relationship. There are other kinds of addictions, to be sure, like gambling, alcohol, or drug abuse, uncontrolled spending, overeating, and all are damaging to the individual and to the couple.

Two authors, both women, tell their personal stories of dealing with infidelity. One, Meg Wilson, tells of her husband's unfaithfulness. The other, Michelle Langley, tells of her struggle with being unfaithful in her own marriage.

Meg Wilson's powerful book tells her own story, with insights from others suffering the infidelities of their spouse. It includes input from other wounded wives, as well as from her husband and others in his situation. Its title is *Hope after Betrayal: Healing When Sexual Addiction Invades Your Marriage*.[10] Here are portions of the book in excerpt form in which Wilson addresses critical concerns, with references to the location of the excerpt in the electronic book form. It is worth buying the book and reading every word.

Who suffers when sexual addiction invades the home? Wilson's perspective begs our attention:

Location 206: Who is hurting the most?
I wasn't the only one hurting. It began to sink in that God was showing me Dave's years of pain. He was a broken man.... My anger cooled. Dave wasn't having fun. On the contrary he'd been living a double life and battling demons since he was eleven years old.

The impact on the spouse is generally catastrophic, but each woman (in this case) reacts or responds uniquely. Undoubtedly there are many more ways to respond, but here are a few of the more recurring ones:

Location 376: What are some typical reactions to the

betrayal?

Point the finger: "At first, I wanted to focus on what my husband had done."

A superior attitude: "My sins are miniscule compared to my husband's."

Hiding: "I wanted to go to bed and never wake up."

Attacking the problem: [Another woman] wanted to "stuff the pain and put all her energy into helping him move forward...to attack the problem like any other—with education and logic."

Revenge: One wife said that her decisions were based more on instinct than on thought. She let her pain do the talking, "All I wanted was revenge...I thought that would make me feel better. I wanted to give him some of the pain he'd given me."

Wilson hits the nail on the head by making it abundantly clear that the wife did not cause the addiction, but the response to the discovery is critical and serves as a wake-up call:

Location 452: What is the wife responsible for?

[The wife]: Although we did nothing to cause our husband's addiction or affair, we are responsible for our reactions. Warning: wounded women are vulnerable to an affair. One bit of attention from the wrong man can be like water to a dry sponge. Our need for assurance is at an all-time high: "If another man is attracted to me, I must be okay."

It would be hard to find a more succinct and compelling definition of forgiveness and enabling than what the author states here—agreeing "to live with the consequences of another's poor choice and give up my right to punish." Powerful!

Location 1182: What is forgiveness after all?

When I extend forgiveness, I'm agreeing to live with the consequences of another's poor choice, and I must also give up my right to punish. The other extreme is enabling, protecting a person from the natural consequences of his or her choices....

Again, the "blame" for sexual addiction lies exclusively with the addict, but a more compassionate view looks at the hurts and pain behind the behavior. Jesus was the ultimate Specialist in dealing with the brokenness beneath the behavior:

Location 1316: How do you think the wife's attractiveness ties into the husband's addiction?

Truth: Sexual addiction starts when men are young boys, before they ever meet their wives. This addiction is not about sex or attractiveness…All addictions are about medicating pain and escaping…deep, emotional hurts…like abuse, abandonment, critical or absent parents, any number of injuries that are too deep for a child to process.

It's human to want a quick fix to any problem. We men are particularly prone to be fixers, and a common mistake after the discovery of an affair or addiction is to say, "It's over, I'm sorry, I said I'll never do it again—why can't you get over it? Just trust me." The sad part is that when trust is broken, the restoration of it takes a long time. It becomes a rebuilding process and that sometimes takes years, or even a lifetime of restoring what was broken.

Location 1404: How can we combat the lies that swirl around us?

The average time for healing is five years…this place of pain isn't constant for those five years…go back to the basics: God loves me; he made me with a plan in mind; I can't work on the plan without him. Then I count the many blessings and look at all the times God was faithful in the past. Truth is the medicine that treats lies...even though my husband was getting help and working on his issues, he could still fall...these men are forever one poor choice away from slipping right back into their addiction.

Again, the perspective on the societal view of sexual addition is compelling. The fear, shame, and guilt that hover over the errant behavior can be devastating. The following two responses capture it well:

Location 1501: Husband's chapter (to a group of wives of sex addicts):
[Husband]: I need to reiterate that your husband's sexual addiction (SA) has nothing to do with sex. It has everything to do with avoidance of pain (medicating) and addiction... [and that] the chemicals released in his body during sexual activity are a way of coping with the "issues" in his life. One reason SA is different than other addictions (alcohol, drugs, food, work, etc.) is the greater havoc and destruction caused on a relational level.

Location 1536: Why didn't my husband tell me about his problem before?
Most likely he believed that you'd walk out on him...One of the differences between SA and other forms of addiction is the shame and guilt...When people admit to being an alcoholic or a drug addict, they're celebrated for their courage in admitting their struggles. That's just not the case for men struggling with SA. Not only do men have a sense of guilt and shame about their addiction, society denies it's even an addiction.

It's easy to fall into the trap of self-blame, the "what ifs" about the wife's own life, appearance, and behavior. It is an issue that must be emphasized over and over until we understand the truth behind it:

Location 1584: What could I have done to prevent all this?
   Nothing ... I can't stress this enough. Your husband's addiction has nothing to do with you. It has nothing to do with how you look, how available you are to him sexually, your personality, your weight, height, or the color of your hair.

   Is there hope for change? How can I believe for it? Wilson outlines it:
Location 1613: How will I know if my husband is getting healthy?
   The first marker of healthiness is honesty. For years your husband has been living a lie [and] on the journey to healing, he'll learn that honesty is essential to his recovery.
   Second, is he growing closer to God? If the guy hasn't started to deal with his heart issues, then it's only a matter of time before a relapse occurs.
   Lastly, are you seeing real change?... the important thing is that he's serious about continuing on the road to recovery.

   Self-disclosure is the key here. Secrets are ghosts that will haunt a person all their life. The Bible says it so well: "Confess your faults one to another and pray for one another that you may be healed." It is powerful when a person says, "This was my fault." Asking and extending forgiveness is a mountain-mover and leads to healing.
   When a partner reveals their faults or confesses their sin, they are doing the right thing. However, confessing is one of the most difficult challenges a person can face. Often they are terrified of the consequences of their disclosure. What if he or she leaves me? What will my friends and family say if this gets out? Will I be a disgrace to my colleagues? Will I lose my job? That fear of the consequences of self-disclosure

is definitely an obstacle. The woman who was caught in adultery and dragged before Jesus felt the awful accusations and condemnation of society and was terrified of being stoned by the angry mob. After dealing with the mob, Jesus said to her, "I don't condemn you; go and sin no more."

When your spouse self-discloses, he or she is giving you a gift, the truth, something that is not done often enough. You may feel hurt or betrayed and thoughts of revenge may try to overwhelm your mind, but if with God's help you can lay that aside and handle with care that piece of inner self that your partner is giving to you, God will give both of you "grace to help in that time of need." Your demonstration of grace will make you Christ-like and pave the way for the true restoration of your marriage.

*Infidelity—A Heavy Burden*

I remember recently listening to a Christian leader tell about the heavy weight of guilt he carried because he had an affair twenty years earlier. He confessed it to his wife, who locked herself in her room, shutting him out for a whole year as she grappled with the heartbreak. She read more than one hundred self-help books and virtually quit eating, losing eighty pounds during that time.

He could have easily rationalized that so many years had passed, that he was a changed man now, but the guilt and need to be honest with his wife was still there, even after twenty years. But her reaction was to shut him out.

It was tough, but her husband took it with understanding, and God finally did a work of grace in her, too. As it turned out they reconciled and remained married fifty years. They both have passed away, but not before they dealt with their issues of guilt, shame, and unforgiveness, and the Holy Spirit's work of restoration wiped the slates clean in both of their lives.

## *The Unfaithful Wife*

I inferred earlier that there are two sides to this coin of cheating on the partner. Secular author Michelle Langley wrote *Women's Infidelity: Living in Limbo: What Women Really Mean When They Say I'm Not Happy*. Langley states that 70 to 75% of all divorces today are initiated by women, most in their late twenties on average, and are most likely to occur in the fourth year of marriage "across more than sixty radically different cultures."

The observation then would be, is infidelity one of women's best kept secrets? Do women seek separation or divorce under the guise of searching for self? Is this all about an identity crisis? Are men being divorced by their wives without ever knowing about their wife's extramarital sexual relationships?[11]

Langley is not a psychologist but rather refers to herself as a "personal and professional development coach." After being happily married for four years and then suddenly feeling "bored and unhappy," she attempted to discover why she had gone down the path of infidelity and began personally researching the matter over a ten-year period. She eventually interviewed 123 women and 72 men in her research. As a result she was able to identify four stages in the pattern of ongoing relationships of many "unhappy" women and their husbands, beginning with a loss of sexual desire on the part of the woman:

> After studying women's sexuality for more than ten years, I can honestly say that many of our societal beliefs about females are grossly distorted and some are completely erroneous. Unfortunately, society's preoccupation with male infidelity and male commitment issues has kept and continues to keep a light from being shined too closely on female infidelity and female commitment issues. The media

has finally begun to acknowledge, albeit to a small degree, the widespread problem of female infidelity. But, to be clear, female infidelity is one of the most prevalent problems that couples are facing today in their relationship.[12]

Langley concludes, "Female infidelity will not only continue to be extremely common, but it will also continue to be on the rise…women are cheating and relationships are ending because men and women lack necessary information. Today's relationship problems are not only solvable, but many can be easily solved—once you understand what the real problem is."[13]

It would therefore seem to be axiomatic and obvious that for every heterosexual man who cheats and has an affair, another woman must be involved. It would also appear that human nature leads both men and women to blame their spouse and justify themselves rather than look inside and find healing, or repair the foundations to their marriage if they intend to find the "bliss" for which they are searching.

Esteeming our spouse better than ourselves may mean self-denial or learning to do something with which we are uncomfortable, which may in fact seem impossible or unjust. When we take that first step toward restoration, we are rebuilding bridges of connection to that person we married.

We do live in a wicked and adulterous generation, as Jesus would call it, and it is our responsibility to commit to faithfulness to God, to our spouse, and to ourselves. Neither men nor women are more prone than the other to unfaithfulness, more inclined to cheat, so let us commit now to finding as many ways as possible to connect with our married partner and be true to them for as long as we live.

## Notes

1. Louie Giglio, *Goliath Must Fall: Winning the Battle Against Your Giants* (Nashville: Thomas Nelson, 2017).
2. Paul Hegstrom, *Angry Men and the Women Who Love Them: Breaking the Cycle of Physical and Emotional Abuse* (Boston: Beacon Hill Press, 2011).
3. American Addiction Center, "Mental Health Disorder Treatment Guidelines," PsychGuides.com, 2019.
4. American Addiction Center.
5. Gary Chapman, "Processing Anger Healthily Part 2," 5lovelanguages.com.
6. Boye Lafayette De Mente, *NTC'S Dictionary of Mexican Cultural Code Words* (Lincolnwood, IL: NTC Publishing Group, 1996).
7. Domestic Abuse Topline Facts and Statistics, "Key Topline Statistics Related to Domestic Violence, Abuse, and Intimate Partner Violence," domesticshelters.org, January 7, 2015.
8. José L. González, *Machismo y Matriarcado: Raíces Tóxicas Que Marchitan La Cultura Latinoamericana* (Chesapeake, VA: Semilla, 2014).
9. George Bell, "How to Prevent Bullying," Stand Tall Against Bullying.
10. Meg Wilson, *Hope after Betrayal: Healing When Sexual Addiction Invades Your Marriage* (Grand Rapids, MI: Kregel, 2007).
11. Michelle Langley, *Women's Infidelity: Living in Limbo: What Women Really Mean When They Say I'm Not Happy* (St. Louis, MO: McCarlan Publishers, 2005).
12. Michelle Langley, Women's Infidelity, www.womensinfidelity.com/adultery_wife.html.
13. Langley.

# CHAPTER SEVEN:

## Nurturing Intimacy with Your Spouse

# 7. RECOGNIZE "BIDS" AND LEAN TOWARD YOUR SPOUSE

### Couples in the Lab—The Gottman Experiment

Dr. John Gottman wanted to know more about how successfully married couples created a culture of love and intimacy and how those who separated from or divorced their spouse squashed it. He designed a lab in 1990 on the University of Washington campus to look like a beautiful bed and breakfast retreat center. He invited 130 newlywed couples to spend the day at this retreat and observed them as they did what couples normally do on vacation: cook, clean, listen to music, eat, chat, and hang out. He made a critical discovery in this study, one that gets to the heart of why some relationships thrive while others do not.[1]

### Bids Throughout the Day

Throughout the day, one or the other of a couple seemed to offer to connect with the spouse in what Gottman calls "bids." These bids take the form of innocent, normal, everyday comments, such as "Oooh, what a pretty bird in that tree!" or "Oops, I can't find my keys," or "Looks like we're running out of milk." They are ordinary, almost-under-your-breath observations. The importance of the matter does not lie in the content of the comment but in the response to it.

For example, let's say that one of the two happens to be an avid bird watcher. One day he or she sees a cardinal land on a tree branch outside the window and spontaneously comments, "Look at that beautiful cardinal out there!" They are doing more than just commenting on the pretty bird. They are, consciously or otherwise, making a bid toward the spouse and looking for some sign of interest or support.

**Responding to the Bids**

At that moment, the spouse has several options:

1. They can ignore the comment (bid) in silence, which essentially proclaims "Can't you see that I'm not interested in your birds? I'm reading the paper, so leave me alone."

2. They can comment positively on it ("Yes, we don't see that many bright red cardinals around here at this time of the year. They sure do brighten up the place!").

3. The spouse can criticize or speak disdainfully of it ("Those dumb birds make such a mess out there; I wish they would disappear.") If you are talking about lost keys, negativity can take the form of, "There you go again; you're always losing something!" By the way, this attitude of contempt is by far the most harmful reaction, a killer.

4. They can explore or investigate the matter ("I wonder if the male or the female is the more colorful bird"). A small learning experience is born out of curiosity.

5. Finally, as in the case of lost keys or needing to buy more milk, the spouse can offer to help by saying, "I'll help you look for them; when do you last remember having them?" or "I'll run down to the market and pick up a gallon of milk."

Gottman says that 3, criticism or contempt, is the worst response and can ultimately become a marriage-breaker.

Likewise, positive affirmation in its various forms, such as in 2, 4, or 5, can build bridges of connection in small but ever-accumulating ways that will ultimately close the distance between the spouses and forge a strong marriage that will stand the test of time. The key is becoming intentional about paying attention when these comments present themselves. When you acknowledge and pay attention to your spouse in this way, you are on your way to success.

In the case of such an innocent comment, the spouse, however momentarily, is making a connection. If a couple "turns toward" one another a dozen times a day, each connection builds an emotional bridge between them. Likewise if the partner "turns away from" the spouse and these bids or offers for connection are ignored or disdained, the couple will inevitably create distance or barriers between them.

Although these bids may seem of minor importance, in reality they reveal much about the health of the marriage. The comments about the bird clearly show that it was of sufficient importance to comment about it and in that way, insert it in the conversation or lay it out there for a possible reaction. The key question is, does the spouse consider it important enough to recognize and respect it? To do so is to affirm or validate the opinion or point of view of the other.

In this study the spouse that turned toward their spouse demonstrated interest and support in their spouse's observations, comments, or opinions. Others did not respond; that is, they turned away from their spouse, not responding or responding only minimally while continuing to do what they were doing before, like watching television or reading the newspaper.

## The Success Rate: 87% versus 33%

These bidding interactions had profound effects on marital well-being. After a six-year follow-up study Gottman's team discovered that the couples that had divorced had "turn-toward bids" only 33% of the time. Only a third of their bids for emotional connection were met.

The couples that were still together after six years had "turn-toward bids" 87% of the time.[2] Almost nine times out of ten, they were engaging with their partner by validating them. This kind of "leaning toward" seems so insignificant, yet it not only signals the direction of the mind and heart of a couple, but it also demonstrates how we can intentionally practice turning toward our partner and thus incline our hearts toward one another in various ways every day. This bridges the gap between us and our spouse, and it is worth it.

In fact, by simply observing these types of interactions, Gottman and his team can predict with up to 94% certainty whether couples—educated or not, rich or poor, childless or not—will be broken up, together and unhappy, or together and happy years later. Much of it comes down to the spirit couples bring to the relationship. Do they bring kindness and generosity, or contempt, criticism, and hostility?

Just as a mother or father leans down and listens to their child who is calling for their attention, God does likewise. Thus the psalmist says, "I love God because He hears my voice…and bends down to listen" (Psalm 116:2, NLT). We should likewise turn toward our spouse at every opportunity. It will build a bridge toward your spouse and will help you reinforce your marriage.

By the way since learning this key, Cynthia and I now intentionally lean toward each other throughout the day whenever a comment is made. It has become a habit, a positive one, and we can feel the connection growing.

# # 8. LEARN A NEW LANGUAGE

## Adjust to the Differences

In this case we are talking about learning how to communicate effectively with your spouse, learning all about them. It is fundamental for each spouse to learn to adapt to the differences between males and females in spite of a cultural trend today that is attempting to erase those distinctions. A popular book that stands the test of time and illustrates the differences between men and women is titled *Men Are from Mars, Women Are from Venus: The Classic Guide to Understanding the Opposite Sex*, by John Gray.[3] Also, *The Tale of Two Brains* is a highly entertaining YouTube video clip by Mark Gungor with more than six million views so far.[4] It has been popular for a number of years. In it Gungor explains male/female differences in a fun way. Check it out!

On one occasion we traveled to another country. Some friends there related this account to us. An American man somehow connected on the Internet with a beautiful native woman from the country we were visiting. He was enthralled with her and made arrangements to visit her in her home context. They met and in spite of the language barrier—he did not know her language and she didn't know English—he was head over heels in love and decided to marry her. According to the custom of that land, he asked for counsel from her pastor, who said that it wasn't wise to marry without being able to communicate and recommended that they wait six months and learn each other's language.

Against that sound advice, he was convinced he should marry her right away, and he did. Within days, they went to see the pastor again. The American had a black eye and bruises on his cheek and was visibly upset. "What happened?" asked the pastor. "I don't know!" "Well you must have done or said something," replied the concerned pastor. The man then said, "I started to say, 'Honey, let's...and she hit me!' The pastor pointed out: "In our language, that means, 'I'm going to hit you', so she hit you first!"

It certainly illustrates how often a man and a woman are shaped in different ways culturally and must learn to speak the language of the spouse if they are to avoid trouble.

## Chapman's Five Love Languages

When dealing with the issue of getting on the same page, or speaking the same language, we can do no better than the book by Gary D. Chapman, *The Five Love Languages*. This book has been translated into fifty languages and has been a steady best seller for the past twenty-six years; as of this writing it is ranked number 11 on the *New York Times* list of best-selling advice books. It is by far the oldest book on the list. In almost every year since it was first published in 1992, it has increased its sales over the year before. More than twelve million copies have been sold.[5]

My wife and I have done marriage and family seminars in twenty-one countries, sometimes in a local setting, sometimes on a national scale, in churches or citywide settings. It is surprising how many people are familiar with the book. In fact, in a recent seminar with about 125 pastors and their wives in Ciego de Avila, Cuba, one pastor told of the awful time they were having in their marriage. He came across *The Five Love Languages* book, and they gave testimony in the seminar about how it radically changed their marriage. I wasn't so much surprised at the result, but that he had a copy of the book in his home!

The book and sequels to it (*The Five Love Languages for Singles, The Five Love Languages for Men, The Five Love Languages of Children, The Five Languages of Appreciation* [instead of "love," for obvious reasons] *in the*

*Workplace*) outline five ways to express and experience love or appreciation that Chapman calls "love languages": receiving gifts, quality time, words of affirmation, acts of service, and physical touch. You can go online and download the book and take the Love Language Personal Profile quiz to see what are your primary and secondary love languages. Cynthia and I did, many years ago, and then recently we retook it. We'll tell you about that shortly.

The idea is simple: Break down and decode the different ways in which people communicate with their partners so they can finally take the mystery out of what the significant other *really* wants and hopes for.

So what exactly are these languages of which Chapman speaks? What are these five ways of expressing and experiencing love and encouragement?

According to Dr. Chapman, there are five universal ways that all people communicate and interpret love. Through his more than thirty years of couples counseling, Dr. Chapman has noticed specific patterns in the way partners communicate—and it turns out that most people express and interpret love in the same five ways, according to his observations.

These expressions and interpretations are his famous five love languages. Dr. Chapman firmly believes that each person has one primary and one secondary love language, and he theorizes that people tend to give love in the way they prefer to receive love. Since we don't all have the same preferences as our partners when it comes to giving and receiving love, this is how relationships can get sticky. But by understanding our partner's inherent love language, we can begin to remove walls of separation in our romantic lives. Here they are.

*Words of Affirmation*

One way to express love emotionally is to use words that build up. Solomon, author of ancient Hebrew wisdom literature, wrote, "The tongue has the power of life and death" (Proverbs 18:21, NIV). Many couples have never learned the tremendous power of verbally affirming each other. Verbal compliments, or words of appreciation, are powerful communicators of love. They are best expressed in simple, straightforward statements of affirmation, such as
"You look sharp in that suit."
"Do you ever look incredible in that dress! Wow!"
"I really like how you're always on time to pick me up at work."
"You can always make me laugh."

It is especially important to affirm not just appearances but especially to affirm values as well. Notice that in one statement above the spouse is placing value on, and affirming, "that you are always on time to pick me up." You know that as a result, the spouse who hears those words will have a greater incentive to continue to be punctual.

Maybe we won't always look beautiful or handsome or dress nicely, but we can always be kind, punctual, relaxed, gracious, helpful, generous, thrifty. Those are virtues that underscore who a person really is inside and not just how they appear on the outside. Looks are important because, as the Bible points out that "people look at the outward appearance," but then adds "but the LORD looks at the heart" (1 Samuel 16:7, NIV).

So when we also look at a person's heart and affirm it, we speak God's words into their inner self. Psychologist William James said that possibly the deepest human need is the need to feel appreciated.[6] Words of affirmation will meet that need in many individuals.

## Quality Time

Quality time means giving someone your undivided attention. It doesn't mean sitting on the couch watching television together. When you spend time that way, Netflix or HBO has your attention— not your spouse. Quality time is sitting on the couch with the television off, looking at each other and talking, devices put away, giving each other your undivided attention. It means taking a walk, just the two of you, or going out to eat and looking at each other and talking.

Time is a precious commodity. We all have multiple demands on our time, yet each of us has the exact same hours in a day. We can make the most of those hours by committing some of them to our spouse. If your mate's primary love language is quality time, he or she wants you to be with them, spending time together.

## Receiving Gifts

Almost everything ever written on the subject of love indicates that at the heart of love is the spirit of giving. All five love languages challenge us to give to our spouse, but for some, receiving gifts, visible symbols of love, speaks the loudest.

A gift is something you can hold in your hand and say, "Look, he was thinking of me," or, "She remembered me." You must be thinking of someone to give him or her a gift. The gift itself is a symbol of that thought. It doesn't matter whether it costs money. What is important is that you thought of him or her. And it is not the thought implanted only in the mind that counts but the thought expressed in securing the gift and giving it as the expression of love.

Our oldest daughter, Esther, is amazing in this area. When she goes out to buy someone a birthday card, Father's Day, Mother's Day, or anniversary card—whatever the occasion, she will spend a lot of time searching for the right card that says exactly what she wants to communicate. It is a moving experience to get a card from her. Just minutes ago, in fact, she came to tell me that someone she had met at the Banana Republic clothing store at the mall where she works came by the store yesterday and gave her a little note and gift card telling her how much her smile and joyful attitude meant to them. They were speaking her love language—and she was flying high!

But what of the person who says, "I'm not a gift giver. I didn't receive many gifts growing up. I never learned how to select gifts. It doesn't come naturally for me." Congratulations, you have just made the first discovery in becoming a great lover. You and your spouse speak different love languages. Now that you have made that discovery, get on with the business of developing a new language. If your spouse's primary love language is receiving gifts, you can become a proficient gift giver. In fact, it is one of the easiest love languages to learn and the results don't necessarily have to be expensive.

*Acts of Service*

For some, their primary love language is acts of service. By acts of service, I mean doing things you know your spouse would like you to do and that you like doing. You seek to please your spouse by serving them, to express your love for him or her by doing things for them. An act of service person feels loved when they hear the words, "Let me help you with that."

Consider actions such as cooking a meal, setting a table, emptying the dishwasher, sweeping or vacuuming, changing the baby's diaper, picking up a prescription, keeping the car in operating condition, filling it with gas, buying something at the grocery store—they are all acts of service. They require thought, planning, time, and effort. If done with a positive spirit, they are indeed expressions of love.

There are tremendous benefits to meeting the emotional needs of your spouse. If your spouse's love language is acts of service, then actions speak louder than words.

*Physical Touch*

We have long known that physical touch is a way of communicating emotional love. Numerous research projects in the area of child development have arrived at that conclusion. Babies who are held, stroked, and kissed develop a healthier emotional life than those who are left for long periods of time without physical contact.

Physical touch is also a powerful vehicle for communicating marital love. Holding hands, kissing, embracing, and sexual intimacy are all ways of communicating emotional love to one's spouse. For some individuals physical touch is their primary love language. Without it, they feel unloved. With it, their emotional tank is filled and they feel secure in the love of their spouse. To this person, nothing speaks more deeply than an appropriate touch. That doesn't mean only in the bedroom but everyday physical connections, like hand holding, hugging, kissing, a lingering hand on the back, or any type of reaffirming physical contact is greatly appreciated.

I think all of us know people who really can't talk without using their hands. It is how they interact with the world. A person who speaks the language of physical touch isn't necessarily an over-the-top toucher, but having a little physical contact does make them feel safe and loved. Likewise any instance of physical abuse is a total deal breaker.

For my wife, Cynthia, physical touch is second on her list. Unfortunately for me, it is at the bottom of my list of five. What does that mean? It means I have to be very aware of my tendency to avoid or underappreciate actions like hand holding or hugging. If it's important to her, then I need to take more initiative in actions that involve physical touch.

Considering I'm originally a non-hugger, non-hand-holder, non-kisser (greeting-type kiss on the cheek—we're talking social graces, not romantic or sexual touching, which falls into another category), I thought it was hilarious that God directed us to ministry in Argentina for over a decade, where everyone greets everyone, both men and women, with a kiss on the cheek or both cheeks if you are from the western side of the country. It's like a big Italian wedding, godfather style! It has helped me some, and Cynthia is doing her part to show me the way, too, but it definitely is not my love language. It's a foreign language I am trying to learn.

Again, the key is how important it is for my wife that I take her hand while we walk. It is important for me to learn how she expresses and experiences love. Touch requires little time but much intentionality, especially if physical touch is not your primary love language and if you did not grow up in a "touching" family. Sitting close to each other as you watch your favorite television program requires no additional time but may communicate your love loudly. Touching your spouse as you walk through the room where he is sitting takes only a moment. Touching each other when you leave the house and again when you return may involve only a brief kiss or hug but will speak volumes to your spouse.

Once you discover that physical touch is the primary love language of your spouse, you are limited only by your imagination on ways to express love.

One additional and important alert: obviously each child is different and develops their love languages early. Both you and your spouse developed your own love languages well before you ever met, while you were babies or adolescents. In one of Chapman's books titled *The Five Love Languages of Children*, he stresses the value of learning each child's love languages and treating them uniquely according to their language. If the child is a toucher, an appropriate hug, pat on the head, or holding of the hand means everything to them.

I saw a video clip the other day of a schoolteacher who hugs or fist bumps every one of her children as they come into the class every day. Not everyone will get the same "strokes" out of it, but for those kids for whom physical touch is high on the list, it is a game changer. In fact there are several videos like that, and they are fun to watch.

If the child is strong in words of affirmation, then how you speak to them (not harshly but kindly and with affirming words) will make a huge difference in their formation. Conversely, if such a child hears harsh words demeaning them, they will shrink back and close up.

If the child values quality time, perhaps just sitting by them while they color or paint or draw pictures is all they need to feel the warmth of love.

If their love language is acts of service, you might say, "Johnny, would you go over to that book shelf and find two books—the new one, *The Wonderful Things You Will Be*, and an older one, *The Adventures of Huckleberry Finn*, and bring them to me?" That child will feel loved because he can do an act of service that makes him feel positive about himself. Perhaps, for this child, it would be meaningful for the teacher to say, "I see you got finger paint on the table. Let me clean that up for you while you wash your hands." If it works with children, how much more will it work with your spouse?

Couples are both grown-up children, each with its own unique configuration of personality, strengths, temperament, intelligence, wit, giftedness, and aptitudes. It is worthwhile and should be a lifetime of discovery to learn all about that person to whom you are now married.

## A Surprise Discovery

When Cynthia and I retook the five love languages test online, our results came back immediately in order of priority. We remembered from our first test years ago that words of affirmation was number one for both of us, and that has not changed. But this time we looked for what was 2 and following for each. My 2 was acts of service and Cynthia's was physical touch.

As we talked about the survey's significance to us, I had a mini-revelation. Cynthia is very self-reliant, helpful, and quite willing to do whatever tasks there are to do. If she comes from the store with bags of groceries, she will try to bring them in all at once, not wanting to bother me, and I will say, "Cynthia, don't carry those all by yourself. I can help."

Now I don't win any points for doing acts of service. It is something that is part of my wiring. So when I saw the test results, I could immediately tell that our styles were clashing. Cynthia doesn't want to bother me to do what she can do herself, which makes her feel confident and good about herself, and I want to help her, which makes me feel good. As soon as I saw the clash of essentially positive love languages, I had some insight. I asked for a heart talk, which we will explain later.

I shared with Cynthia that when she does things for herself that I would have enjoyed doing for her, I have a feeling of helplessness, of uselessness, as if I'm somehow not being the helpful husband I want to be. They are just my feelings, but feelings are always valid as signals of something going on inside us that requires attention. We concluded the discussion by her agreeing to let me help. In that way she is letting me operate in my second love language, acts of service. We both win. I love that she is self-reliant, but when she lays that aside and allows me to act in one of my areas of strength, it works well for both of us. It's a win-win.

It is so important not only to "know thyself," as the ancient philosopher Socrates admonished us, but to know our spouse as well and use that knowledge to grow closer to each other. That's what love is all about.

# # 9. INCLUDE YOUR SPOUSE IN DAILY DECISIONS

**Mutual Decision Making Strengthens Relationships**

Just asking, "What is your opinion?" and listening strengthens any relationship. When we were children, it made us feel grown up to hear dad or mom say, "Son, what TV program would you like to see?" or "Sweetheart, what game would you like to play tonight?" It builds self-esteem as we grow up and reinforces it when we marry and raise a family.

My wife and I were having lunch last week in Pho Kim, our favorite little Vietnamese restaurant here in town. I was eating my special soup when I heard a family come into the restaurant, and before I looked up, I heard the mom say to one of the kids, "Where do you want to sit?" There were only about seven or eight tables to choose from, and normally a parent will make the choice: "Here, sit here."

But the child chose the table, and I took the opportunity to compliment the mother, recognizing how effective a tool it is to allow the children to make choices. It helps children to learn the value of their point of view and how and why to make good decisions. She seemed to appreciate the words of affirmation.

It's easy to "just decide," and sometimes it is unavoidable, and it takes more effort to include the other person in the decision-making, particularly our spouse. "Where would you like to go for lunch?" or "How much should we give in the special missions offering?" or "What would you like to watch on television tonight?" These are all questions that include the other person's viewpoint. It builds bridges to them because it says to them, "Your opinion matters to me; I want to know what you think." As I have been more intentional about this with my wife, I have discovered many fresh ways of looking at things, ways I hadn't thought of before. They make sense. Her views make the picture clearer for me.

## Is Money the Root of All Evil?

No, money is not the root of all evil but the love of money certainly is.

Likewise one of the most important areas of decision-making that significantly affects couples is that of financial decisions. Money issues include how to spend, how to save, who controls, how much is too much, declaring bankruptcy, overspending on credit cards, or defaulting on loans. It is one of the most common issues in counseling.

In a fascinating article, "Cheating Isn't Always about Sex," by news writer, author, and relationship columnist Ashley Papa, the writer underscores how problematic is the issue of family finances:

> Cheating on a significant other isn't always about sex. There's another type of infidelity that is less talked about and harder to spot, yet has the same, damaging effect as any other type of betrayal: financial infidelity. And, according to a new Smart About Money survey, the number of people who are financially unfaithful is on the rise. Among those couples who have ever combined finances, two in five (42%) have committed some sort of financial deception. "That's up noticeably from two years ago," Ted Beck, president of the National Endowment for Financial Education, told Fox News. "When people in relationships are financially unfaithful, it can include things like hiding purchases,

hiding bank account statements, taking things from the mail so their partner or spouse does not see, keeping cash, or even having a credit card the other party doesn't know about." Financial infidelity can be as severe as lying about the amount of debt one partner brings into the relationship or about the income he or she makes. It usually goes unnoticed until the unassuming partner finds out on their own through a discovered bank statement, a questionable purchase, or the like.[7]

If you have dug a hole of non-self-disclosure, and that's a nice way of saying, if you've been making all the decisions on your own, maybe it's time to sit down and lay it all on the table. Confess what you need to confess, ask forgiveness, and start all over by including your partner in every decision. It builds trust.

I am pleased to see several presentations for young children that emphasize four fundamental aspects of making decisions regarding the wise use of money. Almost without exception they underscore these four concepts that inevitably involve money: how to save, spend, invest, and donate the money you have. Many teens or adults have no clue when it comes to ways to properly administer their income. Even having a small allowance, perhaps a few dollars, can provide a learning opportunity for the children. Even so, every adult should make a priority of mastering these four fundamental concepts regarding finances. Why not sit down with your spouse and tackle them? You'll be happy you did!

**Humility, a Star Quality**

It takes humility to include the partner when it seems easier to just decide, but according to surveys, humility is the star quality that human beings look for in others, especially in their leaders. According to an *American Way* magazine survey of a few years back[8] the number one quality employees look for in their boss or CEO not surprisingly is humility. If we look for it in our CEOs, how much more important is humility in the marriage. Kindness is what we express to others, while humility is our view of ourselves and others.

For example, it's common among macho males to brag, "I hate shopping." But humility might encourage you to try doing with your wife as you would like her to do with you. If she hates going to football games, then it's her turn to say, "I'm going to find out why my man loves sports so much!" It will widen your personal horizons and create common ground for you both. Every time you build relational bridges and create common ground, you help cement the marriage.

Guys, here are a few helps if you hate shopping but love your wife.

1) See it as a learning experience. Trust me, wives love it when their husbands go with them to buy something at the supermarket or mall. If they are shopping for clothes, women like to look nice for their husband, family, and friends. Find out why.

2) Go with her to listen and affirm her good choices or taste. Give input but do so positively, not critically.

3) Discuss with her in advance reasonable and mutual limits for spending.

4) Take advantage of the opportunity to talk about boundaries for spending but stay in the "yes" mode as much as possible. Don't just talk about what limits you, but what you/he/she can do together. These activities will stretch you and draw you nearer to your spouse.

It isn't necessary to be controlling about spending money. Talking about it, setting boundaries, creating a "yes" approach to paying, spending, and investing while being prudent and not overextending can alleviate feeling a need to control.

## Notes

1. Emily Esfahani Smith, "Masters of Love," *The Atlantic Monthly*, June 12, 2014.
2. Esfahani Smith.
3. John Gray, *Men Are from Mars, Women Are from Venus: The Classic Guide to Understanding the Opposite Sex* (New York: Harper Collins, 1992).
4. Mark Gungor, "The Tale of Two Brains," www.youtube.com.
5. Gary Chapman, *The 5 Love Languages: The Secret to Love That Lasts* (Chicago: Northfield Publishing, 2015).
6. Chapman.
7. Ashley Papa, "Is Your Partner Financially Faithful? Why Cheating Isn't Only Sexual," Fox News, March 13, 2017, https://www.foxnews.com/health/is-your-partner-financially-faithful-why-cheating-isnt-only-sexual.
8. Robert McGarvey, "Field Guide to the New CEO," *American Way*, 2004.

# CHAPTER EIGHT:

## Emotional and Spiritual Intimacy

### # 10. PRAY TOGETHER

**Prayer, Oxytocin, and the Brain**

Dr. David Stoop is the founder and director of the Center for Family Therapy in Newport Beach, California. David is also an adjunct professor at Fuller Seminary and serves on the executive board of the American Association of Christian Counselors. He is a Gold Medallion-winning author, writing more than twenty-five books.

Stoop points out that "praying stimulates the same part of the brain that sex does." Clinical research has demonstrated it to be so. It is no surprise then that praying is included in the oxytocin-producing list mentioned above. Did you think that praying together was just a ritualistic, go-through-the-motions practice? On the contrary, when we pray together, we not only draw nearer to God but also draw nearer to each other. We are bonding. Have you heard the term "uniting or agreeing in prayer"? Yes, we do agree in prayer, but we also bond with each other while praying.

I find it fascinating that in the last several decades, researchers are exploring the distinct brainwave patterns during prayer. Dr. Andrew Newberg, one of the foremost researchers in the field of neurology and spirituality, is the director of research at the Jefferson Myrna Brind Center of Integrative Medicine at Thomas Jefferson University and Hospital in Philadelphia, Pennsylvania. He has done empirical studies on brain functioning among a variety of spiritual practitioners ranging from Catholic nuns engaging in "centering prayer" to Pentecostals praying in tongues.

According to an article, "Faith and the Brain," in *Leadership Journal* (February 21, 2016), "the results of his work and others have confirmed that the human brain is 'hard-wired for faith.'"[1] Repeatedly neuroscience shows that prayer does make a noticeable difference in the physiological functioning of the brain.

So the concept of the release of the neurotransmitter oxytocin during prayer is scientifically verifiable. As a bonding element, it is vital to our spiritual and relational lives to practice prayer, not only to draw closer to God but to draw closer to one another as well. As the old saying goes, "The family that prays together stays together."

A word of caution: be aware that the release of oxytocin during prayer, while having a positive effect in married couples, can also create a danger zone when praying for someone of the opposite sex. The physical element (holding hands, laying on of hands, etc.) and any emotional expressions (tears, tenderness, remorse) can awaken unwanted feelings that can quickly sabotage a relationship. Such gestures can unwittingly bond you emotionally to someone of the opposite sex.

## Be in Agreement with Your Spouse While Praying

Interestingly, one Bible verse captures the two-and-one theme talking about prayer: "If two of you on earth agree about anything they ask for, it will be done for them by my Father in heaven" (Matthew 18:19, NIV).

Learning to agree with your spouse in presenting to God what you can ask from him on any given day can be liberating for any couple.

When we are not doing seminars in other countries, Cynthia works as a marriage therapist, driving to Branson, Missouri, a town about a fifty-minute drive from our home.

Before she leaves, I pray with her for the challenges of the couples that arrive at the counseling center from all over the United States. The couples are there because they are in crisis and on the verge of divorce. Of course, because of confidentiality, I don't know the names of the people whom she counsels, but I do know some of the basic issues, and as I pray for her, the co-therapist, and the couple or couples, I become a participant in the outcome. The counselors there know that the successes don't happen because of their training, technique, or superior knowledge but by depending on the miracle-working Spirit of God.

So Cynthia and I become a team, becoming part of the solution to those marriages in crisis and seeing an impressive turnaround success rate. Along with the other therapists on the team, we participate in the outcome when we participate in prayer. So what do you want to turn out well today? Pray together and see what happens.

# # 11. PLAY TOGETHER

**On Having Fun: Is God a Killjoy?**

On the site 412teens.org, the following was posted:
Why can't Christians have fun? Is God a cosmic killjoy?

Sometimes there's this image of God floating around that portrays Him as some kind of cosmic killjoy. Joy and laughter get labeled as irreverent and thrown out as shallow and immature at best, or sinful at worst. After all, He's God, right? He rules the universe. We are nothing compared to Him. Maybe, just maybe, if we balance our lives right, pray the right thing, do the right thing, and generally act all quiet and holy, He won't get mad at us. Right? Maybe if we're careful, we'll avoid getting stepped on by God's peevishness. Right? Hmm... maybe not so much.

Here's the thing: While this idea of a cosmic killjoy god is true for a lot of religions, it is not the God of Christianity. In fact, while many religions make holiness and pleasure to be mutually exclusive, Jesus "came that [we] may have life and have it abundantly" (John 10:10). Not only did God present a way to new life through Jesus, but Jesus also showed us how to live that life.[2]

**Let the Children Play**

Let's face it, in most cultures, unless children are reduced to a meager existence like begging or child labor, they usually find ways to play. They play with friends, siblings, objects, or animals, or they explore their imaginations to find entertainment wherever they can. It's part of the childhood experience.

Unfortunately for many, life as a youth or adult has its besetting restrictions and tangles, and soon play, fun, and enjoyment are replaced with boredom, drudgery, obligation, and disillusionment. For many that joyless existence can easily translate into a similarly tedious marriage.

Sadly, faith and religion, which should lift the soul and provide refuge from this drudgery, becomes a casualty as well. Religion seems like just a set of rules; church is boring and some don't enjoy it. That's the common concept. For some reason, some Christian beliefs, and in fact many religions, have squashed the idea that believers should have fun. To some, play and fun have no part in religion. They seem unholy, contradictory to piety.

## Finding the Joy

Biblically, however, as we have seen, this idea does not hold up. God is a joyful God who rejoices over his people and commands us to "rejoice in the Lord always, and again I say, rejoice" (Philippians 4:4, KJV) and God "richly provides us with everything for our enjoyment" (1 Timothy 6:17, NIV).

Interestingly for Jesus, his most intense experience, his suffering on the cross and all the anguish surrounding it, was faced with joy because of what lay beyond it. "For the joy set before him he endured the cross, scorning its shame, and sat down at the right hand of the throne of God." Even in his crucifixion, Jesus was motivated by joy. Likewise we can face life at its toughest with the same joy, as James 1:2 (NIV) encourages us to do: "Consider it pure joy, my brothers and sisters, when you face trials of many kinds."

Since the "joy of the Lord is your strength" (Nehemiah 8:10, KJV), it is logical and reasonable that joy and fun should be an integral part of the human experience and that play should be an expression of our joy. Here are some suggestions.

Set aside specific times for play and enjoyment. Set a date night or some activity intentionally designated for fun. Remember that God, who "does not slumber or sleep," still set aside one day to "rest from his work" and commanded us to do the same. We gather with other believers to worship, and we make time for our family. There is more to life than working and/or making money.

One of my favorite memories was driving on General Paz, a highway that circles the west side of Buenos Aires, Argentina. For several miles, General Paz has acres and acres of trees and grass, playfields all welcoming families to have fun. On any given weekend in the summer, literally thousands of families could be seen picnicking, playing soccer (football/futbol), or just lying around on blankets on the grass.

Not just on weekends—oh no! It seems like everyone takes one month of the summertime, usually January or February (being in the southern hemisphere), and goes on vacation. In a family sense it is an excellent antidote to work and the everyday chores of life. In the eleven years we lived there, though staying busy in our work, we looked forward to those summer months the kids had off from school and could join us in exploring the wonderful country we lived in.

Do something together that you've never done before, like visiting museums, exploring caves, watching an outdoor play or a live puppet show, witnessing a historical exhibition, going to a race car event or exhibit, a ballet, a zoo, an old mansion tour, an art gallery, or a carnival ride. It costs very little to go to the beach, trail hike in the woods or mountains, or take an art painting class like my wife did a couple of weeks ago when visiting our granddaughter in New Mexico.

If you have kids, ask them what they would like to see or do. You might be surprised how much fun you can have while you build special memories with the family. Open yourself up to new experiences. Let's enjoy the journey.

## # 12. CONNECT BY TALKING FROM THE HEART

Marriage counselors tell us that one of the top complaints people have about their marriage is a breakdown in communication. For whatever reason, some couples quit talking to each other. The fact is that words in the form of affirmations, compliments, asking questions, offering kindness and love, and even expressing humor, can be strong, bridge-building connectors between two human beings, particularly married couples.

## The Simple Power of Talking and Listening

Did you know that there are verifiable interactive studies demonstrating that two complete strangers can bond with each other by talking through a list of questions and responding to the other person? I quote from *Ask a Counselor: How Do We Keep Our Marriage Strong in Strange Circumstances?* by Kay Bruner (February 26, 2015). Here is her answer to that question:

> I also have a fun answer for you. I ran across an article in the *New York Times*, called "To Fall in Love with Anyone, Do This." This is based on research by psychologist Arthur Aron, who says, "One key pattern associated with the development of a close relationship among peers is sustained, escalating, reciprocal, personalistic self-disclosure."
>
> Aron's research involved bringing couples—strangers to each other—into a research lab. For 45 minutes, the research subjects would ask a list of 36 questions to one another. Once the subjects had asked each other all the questions (and answered them!), then they'd gaze into each other's eyes for 4 minutes. People reported that at the end of the experiment, they felt as close to the stranger in the lab as they did to their family and closest friends.
>
> Now, Aron says, "the goal of our procedure was to develop a temporary feeling of closeness, not an actual ongoing relationship." However, one of the couples who met in the lab married a year later, and so the legendary status of this list of questions was born![3]

In Mandy Len Catron's *Modern Love* essay, "To Fall in Love with Anyone, Do This," she refers to this same study by Arthur Aron, adding this comment: "Allowing oneself to be vulnerable with another person can be exceedingly difficult, so this exercise forces the issue."[4]

The final task Ms. Catron and her friend try—staring into each other's eyes for four minutes—is less well documented, with the suggested duration ranging from two minutes to four. But Ms. Catron was unequivocal in her recommendation. "Two minutes is just enough to be terrified," she told me. "Four really goes somewhere."[5]
You've already got an actual, ongoing relationship, so I wonder what it would be like if you tried the same list of questions in that context. I don't think it would hurt, and it seems like the questions might fit with several of the principles, Gottman's and others, that we have shared with you already. Who knows? It's an experiment. Try it and see.

Although it would be fascinating to do so, we will not include the thirty-six questions here, as they are easily accessible online under the title of the book by Aron, *To Fall in Love with Anyone, Do This*. However, we did try the experiment. Through a colleague, we gave these questions, translated into Spanish, to several dozen students in a seminary in Buenos Aires and had them carry out the experiment, even though the students weren't entirely strangers. The experiment worked well and thereafter served as quite a conversation opener among the students.

Again, a cautionary note: If communication of this sort works with strangers, it will certainly improve your marriage partnership, but be aware of the potential danger of sharing in a self-disclosing manner with members of the opposite sex in casual settings, the workplace, or in friendship circles. That can be a casualty waiting to happen.

You've seen it on television or in the movies over and over—someone is talking with a colleague about their unhappiness regarding their marriage and personal life, and it isn't long before they are feeling a strong attraction to each other and cross the lines of decency and danger. Beware! Someone once said, "You can fall in love with anyone you spend a lot of time with," and though I can't verify that statement, experiments like this one do suggest that there is a powerful effect in verbally sharing with others. The importance in this activity is closing the distance between one person and another.

How much more effective sharing can be when we invest in communicating with the one to whom we are married.

**Heart Talk and Work Talk**

There is hope. Focus Marriage Institute (formerly National Institute of Marriage, originally the Smalley Institute) developed a communication style that has proven to be extremely effective over the years it has been implemented as a tool for couples wanting to restore their marriage. It is called Heart Talk and is demonstrated in *The DNA of Relationships for Couples* by Greg Smalley and Robert S. Paul.[6]

There are key ingredients in this simple style of verbal connection.

- It focuses on identifying and transmitting an emotional message, not so much expressing ideas and certainly not launching accusations. It can be a great tool when used correctly, and couples who learn the essence of Heart Talk will almost always see a turnaround in their relationship.

- Perhaps we should note here that we are not talking about identifying and expressing emotions as much are we are talking about expressing feelings. It's one thing to say, "When such and such happens, I feel very disappointed," or "That really makes me feel inadequate" as opposed to something like, "You really make me angry when you say that!"

- Heart Talk walks a couple (or any two people in a relationship) through the steps necessary to remove relational roadblocks. Many specialists believe that emotional intelligence (EI) is more important to success in life than is IQ, as we note in the title of Daniel Goleman's book, *Emotional Intelligence: Why It Can Matter More Than IQ.*[7]

This communication style builds bridges and draws two people closer to each other. Primarily it is effective because it is non-accusatory, so the listener is much less inclined to try to defend himself or herself, explain what happened, or attempt to counterattack.

Essentially there are two basic types of communication: Work Talk and Heart Talk. Work Talk is common, ordinary communication that has accomplishing tasks as its goal. Throughout the day we say things like, "Will you pick up some milk at the store while you are out?" or "I'll do the dishes tonight," or "The car is running a little rough. We need to check it out." It is a simple A-to-B process with the goal of achieving results or solving problems.

Heart Talk starts at Point A but has no destination point. Its goal is connecting with the other person. There are number of ways in which Heart Talk is counterintuitive, that is, it goes contrary to typical communication between couples.

*In general men tend to disregard the importance of feelings in the human scheme of things.* In a machismo-saturated world we are acculturated to reject feminine virtues. Perhaps that is why in recent years there has been an upswing in the idea of men "getting in touch with their feminine side." The idea isn't to make a wuss out of you, or even feminize you. It is an attempt to say, "You are human, you have feelings, so be mature and learn about yourself and learn to relate better to other people." There are at least a dozen ways to heed the ancient philosopher's admonition to "know thyself." Why not start now to be a more complete male capable of revealing more of yourself to your wife?

Women may also be conditioned by cultural values and even biblical declarations that seem to project the idea that women are always to yield and be submissive to the male, thus adopting the role as the weaker gender. No wonder the feminist movement has caught a lot of wind under its wings!

*Throwing stones*: Often when we want to solve a relationship problem, we instinctively want to lay the blame on other person—"You really went off the rails on that one!" or "You are so selfish, you only think about yourself!" Heart Talk says, "Let me tell you how I feel [useless, less of a man, humiliated] when that happens." Just put it on the table, don't throw stones. That's why it is counterintuitive.

*The defense: counterattack or hide*: Likewise, when we feel attacked, or feel like someone just threw a rock or launched a grenade at us, we often will want to counterattack, defend ourselves, justify, explain why we did what we did, or try to fix the problem. Some try to run and hide. Again, the appropriate response is counterintuitive— validate the feelings of the other person. Eighty percent of the time being heard opens the door to healing.

*Fight, flight, or freeze*: Psychologists will tell us that humans resort to our favorite of three basic ways to defend ourselves: 1) fight (counterattacking); 2) flight (put up a wall, hide in my cave, use a silent treatment). There is a third reaction called 3) "freeze" (everything is put on hold), but it is less common than the other two. Note that all three are an attempt to protect ourselves and stop the pain.

*Lousy listeners*: Finally, our normal response in communication with another person is to talk rather than listen. My wife describes the two typical people in the conversation as "the Speaker" and "the Speaker-in-Waiting." We can't wait for the other to be quiet so we can say our piece.

The goal in Heart Talk is to focus on the emotional message of the speaker. The listener summarizes by saying, "So what I hear you saying is that you feel . . ." or "That must have been tough for you . . ." These are phrases that validate the feelings the other person is expressing and are powerful relational tools.

After the speaker confirms that the listener has heard correctly, the listener validates the feeling with a simple statement, such as "That must have hurt," or "I hadn't thought of it that way before, but it makes sense." These are phrases that show that the listener cares and validate the feelings that the other person is expressing. They are powerful relational tools.

A caution to men who are fixers: instead of jumping in to fix our wife, ask if she simply wants to be heard. If so, having her feelings validated is a powerful connection for both.

## The Red Warning Light: Not Good or Bad, Just an Alert

In Heart Talk, feelings are always valid. They are neither positive nor negative in themselves but rather are like the red light that comes on in the car when something is disconnected or needs attention, or like the red lights and clanging bells at a railroad crossing that warn that a train is coming. In itself the red warning light or bell is not evil; it's a signal to pay attention to something going on inside me of which I may be unaware.

Feelings (sadness, disappointment, humiliation, unworthiness, frustration) tell me that something in me needs attention. When I put that feeling out on the table, and my partner validates that feeling, connection happens. So there is power in sharing and talking with your spouse. Communication builds bridges. There is a danger in this, however, and this may come as somewhat of a surprise, except I believe we understand instinctively how much truth is in what I am about to say next.

**Beware—Words Can Seduce**

Beware of the power of words to beguile and seduce. Sharing with someone is effective if that person is your spouse but be very careful if they are not your spouse! Sharing with someone of the opposite sex can create undesirable situations and negative consequences, as noted previously. A sympathetic ear can open the door for emotional attachments that are an invitation to unpleasant aftereffects. With the exception of working with a professional counselor, do not yield to the temptation to open up about your marital troubles to others—not your colleagues, other family members, friends, or parents.

Have you ever heard the line, "Lady, you deserve to be treated better than that; if you were my wife, I would treat you like a queen!" It may sound sympathetic, but it is also highly suggestive and should not be entertained. These are seeds that are planted that will only grow to be weeds in your mental, emotional, and marital garden. So put the power of words to good use, not suggestive use; connect with your spouse. Share yourself with him or her, connect emotionally, become a more open and a new you and together become the couple that you were designed to be.

There are numerous ways to share and connect, like dating, shopping together, scheduling fun times with friends, playing games, going on excursions, visiting museums, attending sporting events, going to the opera or orchestra events, attending civic events or school plays. The important element is that when you do things together, especially when you talk, the end result is always positive.

# # 13. ENDURE AND PROCESS SUFFERING WELL

Several months ago I ran across a powerful article by Kevin A. Thompson. This article was originally published on Kevin A. Thompson's blog titled "The Most Overlooked Characteristic of Whom You Want to Marry." An excerpt is printed here, but I recommend going to the blog and reading the entire article.

> There is one vital characteristic you should look for in a spouse but unfortunately, it is often forgotten. Few people consider sickness and suffering when picking a mate.
>
> "In sickness and in health." On two occasions I have said those words with the full confidence that the couple repeating those words actually knew what they meant.
>
> The first occurrence brought a smile to my face. She had endured, and marriage was her reward on the other side of illness. Together they have journeyed through the struggles of a serious disease as boyfriend and girlfriend. Now they would be husband and wife. They knew what "in sickness and in health" meant.
>
> The second occurrence brought a tear to my eye. She had weeks to live. The vow renewal was his gift to her. I almost cut the words fearing they might be too painful. But with a crowd gathered I included them as a testimony to all who would hear them say, "in sickness and in health." They meant it and everyone knew it.
>
> Few people consider sickness and suffering when picking a mate...when our spouse knows how

to suffer, when they don't live in denial but confront the sorrows of life, when they don't live in despair but know how to laugh and cry at the same time, when they offer support and hope in all of life's challenges, when they can see the big picture of life, then, every grief is wedded to hope, every sorrow is matched with love and every hurt is paired with healing.

One of the great guarantees of life is that every person, every couple, will suffer. When choosing a mate, choose someone who suffers well and you will never be sorry. You want to marry someone who can endure suffering with you.[8]

Another example of this point is a story of a tragedy in my family. My sister-in-law was a happy grandmother. Her daughter, Kristina, and son-in-law, Evan, had a happy two-year-old son, Austin. One day Kristina and Evan went to visit her parents, grandma and grandpa, in their lovely home, complete with swimming pool.

They were having a fun time around the house, when—tragedy struck. "Where's Austin?" someone asked. Alarmed, they called out, searched the house, then were horrified to find Austin floating in the swimming pool! Despite desperate attempts to revive him by everyone, including the emergency and rescue team, their efforts were in vain.

No one can understand the kind of heartbreak and gut-wrenching pain that comes from suffering the loss of a child like those who walk through that valley of the shadow. Many years have passed since that horrible tragedy. Today Austin would be a young man were he alive. But how did Kristina and Evan handle that heartbreak? Would they somehow survive, or would bitterness bury itself deep in their soul, urging them, as Job's wife urged Job, to "curse God and die"?

We have kept in touch with our niece and nephew and watched them struggle through, then grow stronger, in spite of the perpetual hurt. The pain may lessen over the years, but it never goes away. A couple having experienced this loss might be tempted to quit, but they found strength in their faith in God, their support for one another, and the love of their extended family and friends who have helped them stay on the right path. Two beautiful daughters have been born to them, and God's grace is upon them all. What if bitterness had set in? What if anger and resentment had taken control of their lives? One can only shudder to imagine the possible fallout.

But Kristina and Evan are stronger today because they have endured—that's a powerful word for us right now. Because they kept their faith intact, loving God, each other, and family and friends, they are stronger. In fact, their church uses them for marriage ministry and grief counseling. They are using their pain to help others.

No one can foretell the future or foresee what crises will come their way. We do know that when crises come, we will want to be able to count on our spouse, our partner for life, to walk with us and stay faithful to us "in sickness and in health."

## # 14. DISCOVER A COMMON MISSION, PURPOSE, OR DESTINY

**Why Do You Exist as a Couple?**

This means discovering what are our roots and basic values as a couple, and what is our reason for being. In short we should consider what is important and a priority for us, as well as what our destiny in life might be.

## Building Your House of Values

This part of the journey toward marital bliss is crucial and should be viewed from three perspectives: past, present, and future. Building our marriage is like building a house. We lay the foundations first, then the structure (walls, floors, roof), then finally we furnish it with appliances, beds, dressers, couches, tables, and decorate or paint the walls and the inside of the house because ultimately it has to accommodate our purpose, which is to live in it. Foundations, structure, and furnishings—each depends on the others and contributes to making the house livable. In short, we are making the house a home.

Our foundations include where we come from, including our ancestors, lineage, heritage, background, and in general our origins and historical conditions.

Our structure might include family values, behaviors, traditions, and priorities, or who we are and how we act as a couple or family.

Our destiny is still being forged, but as we consider a marriage mission statement, we are looking to the furnishings of our future "home." In other words, what will we contribute to make this a better world and those in it better people?

*The Foundation: Our Heritage Tells Us How We Got Here*

I believe couples instinctively pay considerable attention to family background. Our history on both sides of our family and extended family helps make us who we are, to a great degree. Ask yourself: What is our heritage and what are our traditions? What brought us to this point in our lives?

Knowing our ancestry—some refer to it as the "family tree"—can give us great perspective on who we are today. I previously referred to Cynthia's parents, both from Scandinavia and both immigrants to the United States. Her father came from Göteborg, Sweden, and her mother from Frolands Verk, Norway. Knowing that her mother, Thea, left Norway at seventeen to come to find work in America as a domestic in Brooklyn and that her father, the rough and tough guy from Sweden, jumped ship and immigrated illegally and ended up in Flatbush, Brooklyn, New York, shaped Cynthia's life significantly.

Cynthia grew up on Long Island in a context of ethnic "old world" groups like Italian, Jewish, German, Polish, African-Americans, and many others. When her friends in school would ask, "What are you?" they all understood that they wanted to know what country your parents or grandparents came from. Today there is a far greater openness to embracing interracial, transcultural, or interfaith marriages, and those roots go deep. Therefore it is vitally important to know what are the extended family traits that comprise your heritage.

Several years ago our son David worked for months to assemble a coffee-table book of our family lineage. He traced our Nicholson family tree back twelve generations to John Howland, one of the passengers on the *Mayflower*, the first ship to bring the Pilgrims to America. In 2020 the landing of the ship at or near Plymouth, Massachusetts, will be commemorated at their four-hundredth anniversary. Our family has visited that site of the replicas of the *Mayflower* and Plymouth Plantation and read the various historical documents and have found it to be an inspiring experience.

We are especially aware of the specific times when God intervened and one of our ancestors was spared and protected and how they married, what they accomplished, and their unique trajectories in bringing the Nicholson family into being. John Howland fell overboard off the *Mayflower* but was rescued. His future wife, Elizabeth Tilly, just a teenager, lost her parents who died in that first bitter winter, and eventually married Howland and they had ten children! The rest is history.

Just three weeks after my paternal grandmother gave birth to my father in 1918, she died in the great, worldwide Spanish Flu pandemic that killed perhaps 50-100 million people, the worst epidemic in history. My father was subsequently given to his maternal grandparents to be raised, but with the condition that he retain his father's family name, Nicholson, instead of Comstock. As a result, my father was raised in a minister's home, which has influenced the direction of our lives until today.

These twists and turns in our personal history and heritage, like that of Jesus and so many others in the Bible, are crucial to understanding God's design in our lives and his sovereignty in guiding us and leading us to where we are today. Our history and heritage cannot determine who we will be in the future, since our free will is involved in the choices we make along the way, but it can help us see ourselves in a larger perspective. The prophet Jeremiah captures this same perspective, God's view: "Before I formed you in the womb I knew you, before you were born I set you apart" (Jeremiah 1:5, NIV).

Charting the personal family history of each spouse helps us know that God has a wonderful plan for our lives and helps keep us anchored. Our foundation remains solid to this day.

*The Structure: Traditions Keep Us on Track*

Other anchors and stabilizers in our lives that tend to keep us heading in the right direction are family traditions.

As I read through the Old Testament accounts of Israel's exodus from Egypt on their journey to the Promised Land, my attention was drawn to how many times God or Moses commanded the people to "always remember" or "never forget." The people were then given a symbolic action to take, like building an altar at a certain place, or piling up twelve stones after crossing the Jordan River into Canaan, or celebrating Passover to remember their deliverance from Egypt, or presenting a basket of food items to the priest. There were numerous symbolic actions, and the classic symbol in the New Testament is given by Jesus himself at the Last Supper, which we celebrate today in the Holy Communion, Lord's Supper, or Holy Eucharist: "This do in remembrance of me. For as often as you do this, you remember the Lord's death until he comes."

We humans forget, but traditions keep us anchored in the timeless values and truths of history. It's why we bless our food before we eat (gratefulness), or tithe and give generously (it's not all ours; God supplies our needs), or put up gravestones (remember our loved ones and what they contributed to our lives).

Sometimes it is a simple reminder like "We are family." We spend holidays together and solidify our family relationships and build togetherness. Admittedly it is painful to hear of disagreements in families and squabbles on those occasions when family members fight over who will do what, when, and where. But they can and should be joyful occasions.

Our family has two traditions that we observe. At Christmas time, before the big meal that has been prepared for the grandparents, parents, kids, grandkids, and all others, we eat a very simple meal with Norwegian origins, taught to Cynthia by her mother. It is called *ris grøt* (pronounced "reese grit"), which is rice cooked in cream with a little butter added, then sprinkled with sugar and cinnamon. It's a small reminder that there are millions who won't enjoy the nice meal like we will have the next day. Never forget.

A second tradition is that Cynthia will buy colorful, though inexpensive, pajamas for the whole family, which we wear as we pose for our traditional family photo. It's fun and simply says, we are family and we belong to each other. The grandkids are all good sports, and we have had a lot of fun and laughter—especially the year we ordered online from

Made in China and all the sizes were too small and split at the seams when we bent over. I thought we would never stop laughing! But family, fun, and laughter are some of our values as a couple, as we demonstrate next.

### *The Furnishings: What the End Result Will Look Like*

Several years ago Cynthia picked up from Dr. Bob Paul and others at the counseling center the idea of a marriage mission statement. We concluded that it would be beneficial to us to analyze our goals and values as a married couple. We decided to write them down, much like businesses, organizations, corporations, and religious institutions often do. We see their signs and plaques conspicuously displayed on walls, boardrooms, and other visible locations throughout the building. Where I worked for seventeen years in our church denominational headquarters, the mission/vision statement could clearly be seen as we entered the building's main entrance.

A vision or mission statement has the net effect of crystalizing in our minds who we are, what is important to us as an organization or team, and why we exist. Sometimes these declarations need to be tweaked as the company expands or matures as an entity.

So we thought that the exercise of defining our values would be vital to us, and it has turned out to be so. Here is what our simple declaration says:

Our mission is to develop a healthy marriage that models a commitment to Christ-centered godliness that expresses itself in

1. Maintaining high spiritual values;
2. Care for all people but especially for family;
3. A generosity of resources and attitude;
4. Enthusiasm for life; and
5. A commitment to an ongoing development of our personal relationship.

You can see that numbers 1 and 5 are essentially spiritual and growth-related, while numbers 2, 3, and 4 include three family values personal to us. In addition to continued spiritual maturing and closing the gap between us as we grow together, we believe in prioritizing people, especially family, being generous to others, and enjoying the journey and having fun along the way. Obviously this can be reviewed and modified as one goes along, reflecting the growth and maturity of the relationship.

If you want to be more aligned and focused as a married couple, we challenge you to sit down with your spouse and forge a vision/mission statement for your lives as a couple. Print it up and display it where you and others can see it and be reminded of what is important to you in life and what is your reason for being, or keep it on your cellphone, laptop, or desktop as a reminder. Work on it—you'll see how it will help you focus your lives and how the bond between the two of you will grow stronger as a result. It has kept us focused as a couple, and in the process it is liberating to know who we are and what we believe are priorities in life.

# # 15. TIE UP LOOSE ENDS: THE BUCKET LIST

We have all made mistakes in our lives, either by what we have done or what we have failed to do. We have not always lived up to the expectations of others or to our own.

**Keep Making Amends Where Possible**

We have discovered a secret that will keep you current with your partner and those around you as well. If you will make it a goal to keep making amends, asking forgiveness, and repairing relationships as soon as possible after discovering where you have personally failed, you will find that your life will be up to date and you won't need to keep secrets or suffer remorse because of your failure to do the right thing on some occasion.

I call it my Bucket List, but not because there are places I want to visit—we've been to seventy-two countries in our world travels, so I don't need to do that. But I do have a list of those whom I have wronged or who have wronged me, and I don't want to carry that to the last day of my life. I want to settle those accounts. Maybe you should consider the same. To do so will build trust and bring you closer to your spouse and family.

For example, many years ago in high school, I participated in a rowdy "senior romp." I didn't personally vandalize or damage property, but I was in the car with those who did, so I was an accomplice. The weird part was that I was a student leader, and my unseemly conduct was an embarrassment to friends and family alike.

Years later God, with his unique sense of humor, sent me back to that town to pastor a church. The principal of the high school during my senior year was gone, but the former vice principal was still there. Now he was the principal! There was no escaping my responsibility. I was sorely convicted and remorseful, and it came to me that I needed to settle the score and pay my debt to society in general and to the high school in particular. Mr. Lee, the vice principal, represented all of that to me.

I wrote a note explaining my role in the misdeeds and then included a check as a token of my sorrow. I couldn't directly repay those whom we had vandalized, but it was the only way I could say, "I'm really sorry." Mr. Lee was gracious and wrote me a nice note saying that what I had done by writing the note was evidence of maturing as a young adult. I was grateful for his magnanimous attitude. My slate was wiped clean; my conscience was clear. My mental hard drive had its miscues deleted and scrubbed.

Every human has a felt need to erase or delete from his or her conscience that heavy weight of misdeeds and faults we have committed in the past that have hurt others and ourselves. We need a powerful cleansing agent that will wipe clean our conscience of these things. The Bible is clear in its teaching that no human sacrificial system can do that. At best in the Old Testament, the system of sacrificing animals covered the sins, but only the blood of Jesus can cleanse the human conscience from "dead works [the accumulation of past mistakes]." "How much more will the blood of Christ... purify our conscience from dead works to serve the living God" (Hebrews 9:14, ESV). Deleted, erased, expunged, scrubbed, purged—gone forever! No other cleansing agent can make that happen.

In that last couple of years I have had two specific occasions to ask forgiveness or say a belated but important "thank you" (one was thirty years late) for times in the past when I was remiss, unkind, or neglectful. I wanted those wrongs to be righted. My Bucket List includes any wrongful or out-of-place actions that have hurt others that I can make right before I wrap up this life.

Are there wrongs you have done before or after you were married that you deeply regret and that have hurt someone? Did you misbehave or commit harmful, immoral, unethical, or even illegal acts that you know were awful? Have you hurt your spouse in a moment of carelessness or ego stroking on your part? Have you been unkind to parents, loved ones, extended family, or friends? Hard as it may seem, asking forgiveness and making amends can help build trust and keep you on track in your marriage.

**If You Can't Make It Right, Find a Substitute**

Here's the kicker, though. What if that person to whom you were unkind is no longer around? Maybe they have died or have vanished into the caverns of the past. In these cases my recommendation is first, after exploring all possibilities of directly making amends with them, do what you can to find someone—a surrogate grandparent figure, father figure, mother-in-law, someone who represents that person who was harmed or mistreated—and do something kind for them.

If you as a child or adolescent were hurtful to another child, perhaps your best move is to find someone who has suffered trauma or abuse and show them care, kindness, and love. You can always simply say, "I am so sorry that happened to you. I care." In this way you will open the door for your own personal growth and healing.

Carrying that weight of guilt all your life is tough. That's why God provides a way for us so that we can confess (which means to "agree with God or others about") our sins and transgressions and be forgiven. We are also to confess our faults one to another and pray for one another so that we can be healed of that fault.

## Long Overdue but Not Too Late

Recently a friend of mine shared with me how his father served in World War II in the Pacific. He was twenty years old at the time. Like many traumatized veterans, he didn't talk about the things that happened during the war, except to his wife. On his eighty-ninth birthday, his family was gathered around the table when the father said to his wife something like, "Go get the teeth." No one except his wife knew what he was talking about.

The wife went to a drawer and took out some items carefully wrapped in paper. They were teeth, extracted from the mouths of the soldiers he had personally shot and killed in battle. Souvenirs. As he unfolded the extracted teeth, he began to sob, as those personal reminders of killing other men took their toll on his memory and conscience. Remember that in the human brain, trauma has no expiration date. It is not bound by time and can always resurface. It is why healing and restoration are so important.

My friend could only say to his father, "Dad, this is in

the past. God has forgiven you; now it's time to forgive yourself." He did. A year later, he passed away in peace. He could not right the wrong, not even for a surrogate, but he could leave it in the hands of a forgiving God. Having carried the burden of guilt for almost seventy years, he was able to lay it down, accept God's forgiveness, forgive himself, and truly rest in peace.

My wife teaches master's-level courses on counseling for church leaders around Latin America. She recently told me of one student in particular who caught her attention when on the final day of classes, Cynthia made two requests of the students: first, to tell what was their primary takeaway from the class, then what would be their next action step. The question is designed to have the students focus on what they have learned, and more importantly, what God might be speaking to their hearts to do next.

The student who most impacted Cynthia confessed to the class: "I came to take this course fully expecting to learn new ways and techniques to help me be a better pastor and leader. Now I realize how wrong I was in the way I raised my children. I thought I was right, but now I realize how wrong I have been in the past and how hard I have been on them. I'm going home to ask my children to forgive me for how I have treated them, and from now on, I will be a different and better father to them!" That is repentance and change, and surely a new beginning for father and children.

**Pay It Forward**

Has someone blessed you in the past, investing something in you that made possible some forward steps in your life? Someone did for me. A businessman gave me a scholarship in college, and I was remiss in expressing my appreciation. Years later, after it was too late for making amends properly with that person, we sold a house and with some of the proceeds from the sale, we made anonymous scholarships available to that same alma mater. We blessed others as we had been blessed, and the account was settled, at least through these surrogates.

Pay it forward; bless someone who has blessed you. Ask forgiveness for your faults and sins of the past, or find and bless someone, like that grandma in a nursing home who represents your deceased mother or mother-in-law. It might seem like a random act of kindness, but if done wisely, it can help restore dignity to someone else and remove an ugly stain from your past in the process.

**A Debt of Honor**

Not all of being up-to-date has to do with asking forgiveness or making amends. Sometimes it is recognizing that someone opened a door and made possible some sort of progress in your life or the lives of others around you.

We have a Korean pastor friend who leads a large Korean congregation on the East Coast of the United States. His passion is to reach and help children of every nation who are between the ages of four and fourteen years. They call it "The 4/14 Window." The church formed a soccer team, which traveled to various countries for exhibition soccer games in large stadiums with local teams of that country. During the halftime of these exhibition games, team members shared their testimonies of how God had changed their lives.

Our pastor friend has another unique passion, however. In every country he visits, he finds out if there are any military veterans of that country who fought alongside the South Koreans during the Korean War. When he discovers one, he and his Korean delegation meet with that person, and the delegation honors the veteran of that country for being an ally of Korea during the war. In their uniquely touching way, every Korean bows very low to the ground before the veteran as a gesture of highest respect. "You stood by us and we will never forget it, and we honor you for it!" When we owe a debt of respect and honor, paying that debt always makes us stronger people.

## # 16. RESET—A FRESH START AND A CLEAN SLATE

Perhaps some of these accounts have made you realize that in the past, and maybe until now, you have done some unpleasant things, that you have been hurtful and have injured people and generally failed in your relationships. Or maybe you have made progress and now you realize how many things are being uncovered that need attention.

You realize now that what you need is a fresh start. You want to wipe the slate clean. In essence, you need to be born again. God can blot out every last stain in your life and give you a new beginning. You get to start all over. What better way to close the distance between you and your spouse and family.

### Start at the Bottom

How do we start all over? Here's the secret: it's counterintuitive. We all think it is based on how good we are, or at least how much better we are than the next person. God's requirement is that every human recognize that he or she isn't good enough, because all of us have sinned and no one is righteous, not one person. In fact, God takes great pleasure in inviting and making his own project the disreputable ones of this world because then he doesn't have to share the spotlight ("the glory") with any human! So start there—at the bottom, at your worst. The great apostle Paul, who wrote so much of the New Testament, referred to himself as "the chiefest of sinners." He knew he didn't qualify for being in God's family.

One of Jesus' disciples whom he chose was Matthew, a

tax collector. Tax collectors were known extortionists and cheaters. This is what happened:

> Later, Matthew invited Jesus and his disciples to his home as dinner guests, along with many tax collectors and other disreputable sinners. But when the Pharisees saw this, they asked his disciples, "Why does your teacher eat with such scum?"
>
> When Jesus heard this, he said, "Healthy people don't need a doctor—sick people do." Then he added, "Now go and learn the meaning of this Scripture: 'I want you to show mercy, not offer sacrifices.' For I have come to call not those who think they are righteous, but those who know they are sinners." (Matthew 9:9-13, NLT)

See how the religious leaders of that day viewed it? Disreputable, scum—and there were a crowd of them, "many tax collectors and other disreputable sinners." But Jesus made it clear that the ones that he invites were not "those who think they are righteous, but those who know they are sinners." You and I qualify to be included when we agree that we need mercy, not because of how good we are but because our sin makes us highly unqualified. That's counterintuitive!

## Keep It Simple!

So God simplified the matter. He made it easy because he is a just and fair God and doesn't want anyone standing before him on judgment day saying, "It was too complicated; I couldn't do it." That would be unfair. Instead, he says, "My requirement is that you agree with me that you aren't good enough and never will qualify on your own for eternity with me." That's what confessing is, literally "agreeing with." Then you believe and accept that he has done all that needs to be done through the death and resurrection of Jesus, his Son. When you believe it and accept it for yourself, the Spirit of God comes into your spirit, and you then have eternal life.

Others may complicate what God has simplified, but don't be fooled. God is fair and just, and if being born again were more difficult or complicated, he wouldn't be a God of justice. He WANTS you to start all over and be born again! He doesn't want anybody to miss out. And he doesn't want you taking credit for the 99% of salvation that he has put in place so believe and receive Jesus into your life and let God make you a new person. Keep it simple!

**Re-Virginization: Is There Such a Thing?**

When we lived in Buenos Aires, Argentina, years ago we had contracted with a local drug rehab center to have some of their workers come and help us do some yard work for which we would pay them. Cynthia was supervising the progress of the cleanup project, and as she talked with one of the young helpers, she happened to ask him if he had a wife or girlfriend. Cynthia was a bit surprised when he said no, he didn't. Noting her surprise, the student explained: "Before I came to faith in Christ, I was very much a womanizer. It was my life. Now I have repented and started a new life, and at this time, I am in a process of God 're-virginizing' me. I'm starting all over in my relationships with women." It was kind of a rebirth in how he treated the opposite sex and how he viewed himself in the process. He was born again and had become a new creature. "Re-virginization"—a fascinating concept.

Once you've allowed God to make you a new person through Jesus Christ, you can commit to being faithful to him, to your spouse, to your family, and to your friends. You can pledge or promise that things are new and will be different "from now on...."

## Activities That Help You Thrive as a Couple

You already know that praying together is a bonding activity. But you can also welcome the activities that will enhance that new person growing inside you. One great activity is joining your spouse in finding a place where your new life can be nourished. The Bible is clear that we are not to "quit meeting with other believers," so look for a congregation in your community that 1) is friendly and interactive, 2) welcomes the presence of God, and 3) provides a regular diet of spiritual nourishment from the Word of God. It's also great if they have a ministry to couples as a priority in their congregation.

In March of 2018, in an article titled "Does Faith Reduce Divorce Risk?" writer Glenn Stanton makes the following assertion:

> Religious belief and activity—particularly prayer—matter in important ways. They make a deeply practical difference in how husband and wife interact with each other in daily life.
>
> Many Christians believe that the divorce rate among believers is on a par with that of the unbelieving world. That's simply not true—particularly for those who take their faith seriously in both belief and practice. The best research from sociology's leading scholars has established this fact time and again over the last few decades.
>
> Most recently, research conducted at Harvard's School of Public Health reveals that regularly attending church services together

reduces a couple's risk of divorce by a remarkable 47 percent. Many studies, they report, have similar results ranging from 30 to 50 percent reduction in divorce risk. Happily, this holds largely true for white, black, Asian and Latino couples.9

Perhaps this is a good time to put into practice some new activities that will enhance your life and marriage instead of allowing detracting behaviors and attitudes to make you someone you don't really want to be.

One shift in attitude about the new life we all are offered through a relationship with Christ is how we view it. Some see religion and church as boring and just a bunch of rules and regulations. While a few might classify it that way, millions would disagree. Besides, we aren't talking about religion; we're talking about a new life. It can be and is a dynamic that builds us up in our journey through life.

**The Good News in a Nutshell**

Several years ago at Christmas time the workers at our headquarters joined together at a nearby church auditorium for a Christmas celebration. There were about seven hundred of us. The leadership had asked one of our colleagues, a woman, to speak to the group. The speaker told of a trip she and a group of friends took to the Holy Land. At one point the tour guide, an Arab who clarified that he was not a Christian, made this comment: "I have read the New Testament to understand what Christians believe, and I can sum it up in one word—RELAX!"

I admit I was not expecting such a summary as our friend told it. But then the words of Jesus came to my mind: "Come to me, all of you who are weary and carry heavy burdens, and I will give you rest. Take my yoke upon you. Let me teach you, because I am humble and gentle at heart, and you will find rest for your souls. For my yoke is easy to bear, and the burden I give you is light" (Matthew 11:28-29, NLT). Years later the apostle John in one of his epistles reinforces that truth by declaring, "His commands are not burdensome" (1 John 5:3, NIV).

This is good news—rest, easy, light, and not burdensome. This is the abundant life Jesus Christ offers us. God is for us, not against us. This is bliss!

## God's Word - Daily Bread, Not Cake for Special Occasions

One other useful activity these days can be borne on the wings of technology—finding daily direction for your life by reading God's Word. I have an app with a Bible-reading plan (The Bible in One Year) that pops up on my iPad and guides me through the Bible, so I read it from beginning to end in one year. I will guarantee the results: if you engage in the daily reading of God's Word, you will be amazed at the revolution it will begin in you as a person!

By the way, I have been inspired by Cynthia's example. She has read the Bible through thirty-nine consecutive years (with one exception, when she tried a different approach that didn't work for her, so she's reading it through twice this year to make up for it!). She has adequately demonstrated the immense value of this daily activity. Why don't you try it?

## For as Long as You Both Shall Live

Cleave, stick to your spouse and only to her or him, and let no other human being come between the two of you—not parents, kids, coworkers, extended family, friends, former spouses or girlfriends/boyfriends. Work diligently at making your marriage the most stable and strongest possible union as you aim for bliss and the "happily ever after" that God has waiting for you. You will never regret it.

### Notes

1. Robert Crosby, "Faith and the Brain," *Leadership Journal*, February 21, 2016, https://rw360.org/wp-content/uploads/2016/02/Faith-and-the-Brain-Leadership-Journal.pdf.
2. "Is God a Cosmic Killjoy?" Got Questions: Your Questions. Biblical Answers, https://www.gotquestions.org/cosmic-killjoy.html.
3. Kay Bruner, "Ask a Counselor: How Do We Keep Our Marriage Strong in Strange Circumstances?" A Life Overseas: The Missions Conversation, February 26, 2015, https://www.alifeoverseas.com/ask-a-counselor-how-do-we-keep-our-marriage-strong-in-strange-circumstances/.
4. Mandy Len Catron, "Modern Love: To Fall in Love with Anyone, Do This," *The New York Times*, January 9, 2015, https://www.nytimes.com/2015/01/11/fashion/modern-love-to-fall-in-love-with-anyone-do-this.html.
5. "Quiz: The 36 Questions That Lead to Love," June 17, 2015, http://zencaroline.blogspot.com/2015/06/quiz-36-questions-that-lead-to-love.html.
6. Greg Smalley and Robert S. Paul, *The DNA of Relationships for Couples* (Carol Stream, IL: Tyndale House, 2006).
7. Daniel Goleman, *Emotional Intelligence: Why It Can Matter More Than IQ* (New York: Bantam Dell, 1995).
8. Kevin A. Thompson, "The Most Overlooked Characteristic of Who You Want to Marry," August 21, 2013, https://www.kevinathompson.com/the-most-overlooked-characteristic-of-who-you-want-to-marry/.
9. Glenn Stanton, "Does Faith Reduce Divorce Risk?" lifeissues.net, March 22, 2018, http://www.lifeissues.net/writers/stan/stan_06doesfaithreducedivorce.html

# ABOUT THE AUTHOR

Richard Nicholson, an ordained minister, and his wife, Cynthia, have traveled extensively throughout their lifetimes to engage in ministry opportunities. In recent years Richard and Cynthia, a marriage therapist with Focus Marriage Institute in Branson, Missouri, have conducted marriage and family seminars in twenty-six countries.

Richard and his wife, Cynthia, have served as pastors, missionaries, and professors with fourteen years as missionaries in Argentina and Mexico. They continue to travel extensively in Spanish-speaking venues, providing marriage seminars based on principles that are foundational to the Focus on the Family Marriage Institute in Branson, Missouri.

The Nicholson's have a happy family of three adult children, eight grandchildren, and a great granddaughter and reside in Springfield, Missouri.

This book reflects their mutual desire to see marriages restored and redirected toward the "happily ever after" for which so many couples are searching.

Contact Richard Nicholson for speaking, marriage seminars, conferences, or meetings at

richard.nicholson@agmd.org

Richard Nicholson

Made in the USA
Monee, IL
15 August 2025

23464595R00098